BIBLE PROMISES

BIBLE PROMISES

SERMONS FOR CHILDREN

ON

GOD'S WORD AS OUR SOLID ROCK

RICHARD NEWTON

Author of *Heroes of the Early Church*,
Heroes of the Reformation, *The King's Highway* etc.

SOLID GROUND CHRISTIAN BOOKS
BIRMINGHAM, ALABAMA USA

Solid Ground Christian Books
2090 Columbiana Rd, Suite 2000
Birmingham, AL 35216
205-443-0311
sgcb@charter.net
http://solid-ground-books.com

BIBLE PROMISES
Sermons for Children on God's Word as our Solid Rock

Richard Newton (1813-1887)

Bible Blessings taken from 1886 edition by Oliphant, Anderson & Ferrier, Edinburgh, Scotland

Solid Ground Classic Reprints

First printing of new edition March 2006

Cover work by Borgo Design, Tuscaloosa, AL
Contact them at nelbrown@comcast.net

Special thanks to Ric Ergenbright for permission to use the image on the cover. Visit him at ricergenbright.org

ISBN: 1-59925-057-8

PREFACE.

WHEN the Apostle Peter was speaking about these 'Bible Promises,' he said God's purpose was, that 'by these we should be partakers of the divine nature.' This does not mean that poor sinful creatures, such as we are, can share in the divinity of God our Saviour. This is impossible; just as it would be impossible for you or me to take up the water of the ocean in the hollow of our tiny hands.

What the apostle means, by the above language, is, that God wishes us, by the right use of these 'Bible Promises,' to learn to 'tread in the blessed steps of the most holy life' of His dear Son; that we may have 'the same mind that was also in Christ Jesus,' 'and become daily more and more like Him.' This is what these promises are given to us for. And I have written these sermons about them, in the hope that my young friends, who read them, or hear them read, may be helped and encouraged in their efforts to love and serve the blessed Saviour. And if this should be the case, I shall feel abundantly rewarded for writing them.

My heart's desire and prayer to God is, that His blessing may rest upon this book, and make it useful to the lambs of His flock.

RICHARD NEWTON.

PHILADELPHIA,
Sept. 1884.

CONTENTS.

———o———

I.

THE NATURE OF THE PROMISES.

'*Exceeding great and precious promises.*'—2 PET. i. 4.

WE enter now on a new course of sermons for the young. Our last course we called 'Bible Models.' The one now before us, we call '*Bible Promises.*'

In the words selected for our present text we have the description of these promises given us by the Apostle Peter. In speaking of them he tells us that they are—'*exceeding great and precious.*'

These promises belong to you, and to me, and to all who are trying to love and serve Jesus. If God had come and spoken some of these promises to us personally, we should have been sure that *they* were intended for us, and that we had a right to lean on them, and expect them to be fulfilled. God has not done this: but yet we may feel towards all God's promises, just as we should if they had been spoken to us personally. If your father should leave you an inheritance, the money thus left would be as truly yours as though you had earned it yourself. But St. Paul tells us that 'the promises' are our inheritance, through faith (Heb. vi. 12). They are *our fortune* in this world. And we have a perfect right—the right which God has given us—to use them as our own. And so, as we go on examining these promises, we shall be like a miser, when he opens the box which contains his treasures. He finds great pleasure in counting over his gold and silver, and calculating how much his gems and jewels are worth. These 'Bible Promises' are *our* treasures. But they are worth ten thousand times more to us, than all the gold and silver and jewels of the richest man on earth are worth to him.

These promises, the apostle tells us, are—'exceeding great and precious.'

The question now before us is—in what respect they are so 'exceeding great'? They are so in *three* respects. In the first place these 'Bible Promises' are 'exceeding great' *in their*—NUMBER.

The Bible is a book of promises. If any one should begin at Genesis, and go through to the last chapter of the Revelation, and count up all the promises there, he would be astonished to find how many there are! These promises were given to different people, under different circumstances, and at different times, and yet they all belong to each of God's children.

See how many precious promises God gives us, about what He will do with our sins, when we repent of them, and believe in Jesus. In one place He promises that 'they shall be *forgiven*' (Isa. xxxiii. 24). In another He says—they shall be '*blotted out*' (Isa. xliii. 25). Again, He says—they shall be '*put away*' (Heb. ix. 26). They shall be '*covered*' (Rom. iv. 17). They shall '*not be remembered*' (Heb. viii. 12). They shall be '*made an end of*' (Dan. ix. 24). They shall be '*sought for and not found*' (Jer. i. 20). They shall be '*cast behind His back*' (Isa. xxxviii. 17). 'Though they be as scarlet they *shall be as white as snow*' (Isa. i. 18). They shall be 'cast into the depths of the sea' (Micah vii. 19).

Here is an interesting story to illustrate one of God's promises, about the sins of His people. We may call it—

THE CLEANSING BLOOD.

An old blind man, who was very ill, was taken to a hospital in London to die.

He had a little granddaughter, who used to go in every, day to read the Bible to him. One day she was reading the first chapter of the first Epistle of St. John. Presently she came to these beautiful words, and read them out: 'The blood of Jesus Christ, His Son, cleanseth us from all sin.' On hearing this verse read, the old man raised himself in his bed, and said to his little granddaughter, with great earnestness,—

'Is that there, my dear?'

'Yes, grandpa.'

'Then read it again—I never heard such blessed words before.'

She read the verse again, 'The blood of Jesus Christ, His Son, cleanseth us from all sin.'

'You are quite sure those words are there?'

'Yes, *quite sure*, grandpa.'

'Then take my hand and lay my finger on that wonderful verse; I cannot see it, but I want to *feel* it.'

So she took the old blind man's hand, and placed his bony finger on the verse, when he said, 'Now read it to me again.'

With a soft, sweet voice she read, 'The blood of Jesus Christ, His Son, cleanseth us from all sin.'

'You are quite sure these words are there?'

'Yes, grandpa, *quite sure.*'

'Then if any one should ask you how I died, say that I died in the faith of these words—"The blood of Jesus Christ, His Son, cleanseth us from all sin."'

After this the old man withdrew his hand, his head fell softly back on his pillow, and he passed peacefully away into the presence of that blessed Saviour whose blood cleanseth us from all sin.

This is only one, out of a great many promises, that refer to the pardon of our sins. And so there are multitudes of promises that refer to all our other necessities in this life. We are exposed to danger at all times; and there are many precious promises in the Bible in which God engages to protect us in times of danger. We have one of these blessed promises in the seventh verse of the 121st Psalm. Here we read: 'The Lord shall preserve thee from all evil.' And here is a story which shows how this promise was fulfilled on one occasion. We may call it—

DIVINE PROTECTION.

An English merchant, who was a Christian, left home, on one occasion, to go to the city of Bristol, to purchase some goods. On the way he was taken sick. His wife went to nurse him; and as soon as he got better she took him home.

Several years after this, he happened to be present when a man was going to be hung for murder. Before the execution took place, the prisoner beckoned this gentleman to him, and said, 'Sir, do you recollect one occasion, when you were going to Bristol, to buy goods, and were taken sick on the way?'

'Oh yes,' replied the gentleman—'I remember that very well. But why do you ask that question?'

'Just to let you know what a lucky thing it was, that you were stopped on the road. I knew of your going; and that you would have a large sum of money with you; and I had arranged with two of my companions, to rob you on the way, and then murder you to avoid being detected.'

God knew the evil which those wicked men had planned to do to His servant, and He made use of that sickness to preserve him from it.

When we are in trouble from the want of food or clothing, there are many promises that seem to have been made on purpose for us, at such times. One of these is that which God made to Abraham, when He revealed His own name to him as—'Jehovah-Jireh—The Lord will provide.'

How many of God's suffering children have been comforted by this promise!

Here is an incident which illustrates this. We may call it—

JACK'S BREAKFAST.

Jack's mother was a poor widow, who was trying hard to support herself and her little boy by sewing. But she had been sick for some days, and unable to work. Her money was all gone, and there was not a morsel of food of any kind in the house. She did not mind so much for herself; but, 'Poor, dear Jack,—what will become of you?' she asked, as the big tears rolled down her cheeks.

'The Bible says, "The Lord will provide,"' said Jack. He was his mother's little comforter; and the words he had just spoken went to her heart, like a beam of sunshine.

'Are you sure, Jack, the Bible says so?' she asked, as she lifted the child to her lap.

'Yes, I'm sure,' said Jack. 'It's in the hymn I learned in Sunday school. Let me tell you one of the verses:—

'"In some way or other the Lord will provide;
It may not be *my* way,
It may not be *thy* way,
But yet in His *own* way
The *Lord will provide.*"

'There, now, it's true, mamma. God will give us something to eat. I have asked Him, and I know He will.'

It was dark and cheerless, in that little garret room, as Jack and his mother went to bed without any supper. But Jack's words had put new faith into his mother's heart; and when Jack asked her, before falling asleep, 'Mamma, do you think God will send us some bread in time for breakfast in the morning?' her cheerful answer was, 'I think He will.'

Early the next morning, the sun was shining through the attic window of their little room; but it was a knock at the door that first awakened Jack. Eagerly the hungry child watched, as his mother opened the door.

A neighbour was there, with a large plate of rolls. 'I baked more than enough for myself, Mrs. Jones,' she said, 'so I thought you and Jack might like them.'

Between her sobs and tears, the mother told the story of their hunger, and of Jack's prayer. 'Why, it's better than we asked for,' said Jack. 'I only asked for bread, and God has sent us beautiful warm rolls instead.'

Jack and his mother would never forget this precious promise—'The Lord will provide.'

And so, in the first place, we may well say that the 'Bible Promises' are 'exceeding great'—in their number.

But, in the second place, these 'Bible Promises,' are 'exceeding great and precious,' in their—CERTAINTY—*as well as in their number.*

And the *certainty* of a promise is the most important thing about it. If a person, who never keeps his word, should promise to give you, or me, a thousand pounds, how much would that promise be worth? Nothing at all. It is the *certainty* of a promise that gives it all its value. But, in the promises that men make to each other, there is often very little certainty. You cannot depend on them. There is an old proverb which says that—'promises, like pie crusts, are made to be broken.' This is often the case with men's promises. There is very little certainty about them. But it is very different with the 'Bible Promises,' of which we are now speaking. These are God's promises. And He always means what He says. His promises are all certain. We may apply to them the words of the hymn, which says,—

> 'Each of them is the voice of God,
> Which spake—and spread the heavens abroad
> And firmer than the solid poles,
> On which the wheel of nature rolls.'

These promises are the words of Jesus; and He had them in mind when He said, 'Heaven and earth shall pass away, but My words *shall* NOT pass away.' The Apostle Paul assures us that 'all the promises of God in Jesus are *yea* and *amen*' (2 Cor. i. 20). This means that they are all entirely sure, and certain. We may trust them, and depend on them, without a moment's doubt or fear. Here is a little story which illustrates the certainty of God's promises. We may call it—

THE SURE WORD.

An eminent minister of the gospel lay on his dying bed. To a brother clergyman who visited him he said,—'In spite of all I have written, and all I have preached, in the forty years of my ministry, there is but one thing that gives me any comfort now, and that is the promise: "Him that cometh unto Me I will in no wise cast out." Do you think I may venture my soul upon that promise?'

'If you had a thousand souls,' said his friend, 'you might *hang them all on that one promise.*'

Surely that minister believed in the certainty of God's promises. He could have taken up the language of the hymn which says,—

> '"In no wise cast thee out;" the word is spoken,—
> And, Jesus, never can Thy word be broken;
> Here then I lay me down and take my rest,
> Calm as an infant on its mother's breast.
>
> '"In no wise cast thee out;" I live, I die,
> And fearless pass into eternity,
> Leaning on this alone: Thy word is given,
> That word secures my safety and my heaven!'

This shows us how the certainty of the promises secures the salvation of our souls.

But it also gives comfort and happiness to God's people when they are in trouble. Here is a little incident to illustrate this. We may call it—

TRIED AND PROVED.

A good Christian lady was visiting an aged widow woman. She was very poor, and very ill; and yet she was bright and happy. A Bible, which she had used for many years, was lying on the table. Her visitor turned over its pages. In doing this she noticed here and there a verse which had a line drawn round it, while on the margin opposite were printed, in capitals, the letters T. and P. The lady asked her aged friend what these meant. 'They mean *Tried* and *Proved*,' was her reply. 'The promises of God's blessed Word have been my support and comfort, under all my trials. And as I have used them, one after another, and found how true they were, I have put these letters opposite to them, to show that I have *tried* them, and *proved* them. When I first saw myself a sinner, I read that sweet promise, "Come unto Me, and I will give you rest." I believed what Jesus said. I came to Him, and found rest. Then I put T. and P. opposite that promise, because I had *tried* it and *proved* it. When I was left a poor widow, with a family of helpless children, my heart was full of sorrow and sadness. But I read these precious words: "Leave thy fatherless children, I will preserve them alive; and let thy widows trust in Me" (Jer. xlix. 11). Then I committed myself and my children to God's care and protection. *That* promise was fulfilled. Then I put T. and P. opposite to it. Since then I have had many trials and troubles; but I have always found some precious promise of God's Word, that seemed to have been written on purpose to comfort me. And I have never found one of them fail.' They are sure and *certain* promises. And if we only make a right use of them, we shall be able to write T. and P., *tried* and *proved*, opposite them all.

I have just one other story to illustrate the certainty of God's promises. We may call it—

SIMPLE TRUST.

There was an old Scotchwoman named Nancy. She had been a happy Christian for many years. Her home was a lowly thatched cottage, in one of the quiet glens of Scotland. She was now sick, and was quietly waiting for death to end her sufferings, and take her into the presence of that Saviour whom she loved. By her bedside, on a small table, lay her spectacles, and her well-thumbed Bible. She called it 'her barrel and her cruse,' which she said had never failed, and from which she had fed continually on the 'Bread of life.'

A young minister often called to see her. He was a good Christian man, but he did not understand the gospel as well as old Nancy did. Yet he loved to listen to her as she talked of her precious Saviour. And when she spoke of her home in heaven, it seemed very near; and he almost fancied at times that he could hear the glad songs which the ransomed sing there.

One day the young minister put this startling question to the happy saint:

'Well, Nancy, what, if after all your watching, and waiting, and prayers, and hopes, and expectations, God should suffer your soul to be lost for ever?'

The faithful old Christian raised herself on her elbow, laid her right hand on her precious Bible, which lay open before her, and turning an earnest look to the young minister, she quietly said,—

'And is *that* a' ye know about the Bible, mon?' And then, as her eyes sparkled with heavenly brightness, she continued,—'God would hae the greater loss. Poor Nancy would only lose her soul. That would be a great loss indeed; but God would lose His *honour*, and His *character*. Haven't I hung my soul on His "exceeding great and precious promises"? and if He should break His word, He would prove Himself untrue, and a' the universe would rush to ruin!'

How simple! how scriptural! how sublime, was the confidence of that dear old child of God in the *certainty* of His promises! These 'Bible Promises' are 'exceeding great and precious,' secondly—in their certainty.

But thirdly, these promises are 'exceeding great and precious' in their—POWER.

Suppose you and I were on board a sailing vessel. The wind has driven us out of our proper course. We have come in sight of land. We are getting very near to it. It is a rocky coast. The waves of the sea are rolling and dashing upon the rocks, in foam and thunder. We are drifting directly towards them. We cannot put the vessel about, and sail away from the danger, because the wind is blowing us right on shore. Every moment we are getting nearer to those terrible rocks. Before long our vessel will be driven upon them, and be dashed to pieces. Can nothing be done to save us? Yes, there is one thing that can be done. And hark! there is the captain's voice telling the men to do it. Above the noise of the wind and the waves he is giving the command—'Let go the anchor!' He is heard. He is obeyed; and down goes the anchor. It stops the vessel from drifting towards the rocks. Now we are safe. The heavy anchor has gone down among the rocks, and the strong iron cable, fastened to it, keeps the vessel steady. No matter how much the waves dash, or the winds blow, there is power in the anchor to prevent the ship from drifting, and to keep her safe.

And just what the anchor is to the ship, under these circumstances, God's promises are to His people, as they sail over the sea of life. The Apostle Paul uses this very illustration. He says the hope which God's people have, growing out of His promises, is like 'an anchor to the soul, sure and stedfast' (Heb. vi. 19). And this anchor is better than any that our sailors have. No matter how good the sailor's anchor may be, he cannot always use it. If a storm overtakes him out at sea, the water is so deep that his cable is not long enough to reach the bottom, and so the anchor cannot be used. But, in sailing over the sea of life, the Christian never reaches any point where the water is too deep for the anchor of God's promises to reach the bottom, and hold him safe and steady while the wildest storm is blowing. How wonderful is the power of these promises! They are able to comfort, and cheer, and bless God's suffering people, in every time of trouble.

Now let us look at some illustrations of the power of

God's promises. Our first story shows the power of the promises—*in doing good to* ONE *sinner.*

Some time ago, an infidel delivered a lecture against the Bible, in a manufacturing town in England. In his lecture he said that the story of Christ in the New Testament was not true, it was all a fable.

When the lecture was ended, a plain working man, from one of the mills, rose up in his place, and said he would like to ask the gentleman a question.

'Ask any question you please,' said the lecturer.

Then the man spoke as follows :—

'Thirty years ago, sir, I was the curse of this town. No one would speak to me, who had any respect for himself. I often tried to make myself better, but in vain. The temperance people got hold of me; but I broke the pledge so often, that they said it was no use trying any longer. Then the police took me up. I was brought before the magistrates and tried. They sent me to prison. There the wardens tried what they could do; still I was nothing better, but rather worse.

'Thus *I* tried; the temperance people tried; the police, the magistrates, and the wardens of the prison all tried to make me better, but in vain. At last Jesus took me in hand. He spoke to me some of the sweet promises of His word, such as these:—"Though your sins be as scarlet, they shall be as white as snow." "I am He that blotteth out thy transgressions." "I will strengthen thee, yea, I will help thee." "My grace is sufficient for thee." These melted my heart, and made a new man of me. And now, I am a member of the church, and a superintendent of the Sunday school. And the question I wish to ask is this: If the story of Christ is not true, —is a fable, as you say,—then how can you explain that it should have produced so blessed and wonderful a change in my poor sinful heart?' The lecturer had no answer to give; and the working man continued: 'No, sir, you may say what you please, but the gospel *is* the power of God unto salvation.'

This story illustrates the power which the promises exercised on one poor sinner. Here is another which shows how that same power was exerted on a number of persons at once. We may call it—

BIBLE TRIUMPHS.

A Bible reader visited a work-house in London one day. On meeting the superintendent, he said to him, 'Sir, have you any room, in this Institution, where such of the inmates as are bad-tempered and unmanageable are confined?'

'We have, sir,' was his reply; 'and a lot of very hard characters are confined in it.'

'Will you allow me, sir, to go in there by myself? I wish to try if I can't bring them to order, and do them some good.'

'Impossible!' exclaimed the superintendent; 'it is very dangerous to go among them alone. I should be afraid to trust you; I never venture in myself without being armed.'

'Oh! if that is all,' said the Bible reader, 'I am not afraid; I have arms in my pocket. Please, let me go.'

At last the superintendent reluctantly agreed to let him enter. He gave him a private signal, which he was to use if he should find himself in any danger. Then the stranger was allowed to enter the prison of the work-house, and the door was quickly closed behind him.

As soon as he found himself among the prisoners, he drew his arms out of his pocket. They consisted of a sword, not of glittering steel—but the sword of the Spirit, which is the word of God. With the Bible in his hand, he sat down on the nearest bench he could find. Then he opened the Bible and read for about fifteen minutes, without adding a word of his own. The portions which he read were chiefly those which contained the invitations and promises of the Bible. The prisoners listened to him in perfect silence. When he had finished reading, he said to them, 'Would you like me to come to-morrow, and read to you again?'

They said they would be very much obliged if he would do so. He went the next day, and did exactly the same. He kept on doing this, day after day, till he had been there twelve times.

When he went the thirteenth morning, the superintendent said to him: 'You might have saved yourself the trouble of coming this morning, sir, for there is not a single man left in the refractory ward. Every one has come out in a quiet and orderly manner, and they are all behaving themselves perfectly well, among the other inmates of the house.' This was a blessed work. Here was a whole company of people, with disagreeable tempers, and evil ways, led to a better state of mind and feeling, and to behave themselves properly, through the simple reading of God's blessed word. What wonderful power there must be in the truths and promises of the Bible, when we see them producing such good fruits as these! Here is a story that we may call—

THE HEART'S-EASE OF THE VILLAGE.

Heart's-ease is the old English name of a pretty little flower that we call the pansy. This story shows us what power there is in the promises of the Bible to make us happy and useful, no matter what our troubles are.

A Christian lady was spending the summer in a beautiful little English village. She was walking through the village one day, with a young girl, whom she had employed to do sewing for her. As they went along, this girl told her various interesting things about different people in the village. Among the rest she pointed to a nice little white cottage on the other side of the road, and said, 'A good Christian woman lives in that cottage, whom we call "our village heart's-ease."'

'And why do you call her that?' asked the lady.

'Because, although she has had so much trouble herself, she is always so happy and cheerful. We all go to her when we are in trouble; and she talks so kindly to us, and has so many comforting things to say, that we call her—"our heart's-ease."'

The next day, this lady went to the little white cottage, to make the acquaintance of the good woman living there. The following is the account she gives of her visit:—

Her name is Alice Fern. I found her busily sewing on a little child's dress. In the course of conversation I learned that she was a young widow. Her husband was a sailor, and died two years ago, just when she was expecting him home. Not long after her baby died, leaving her all alone in the world.

'How much trouble you have had!' I said to her.

'Yes,' she replied, 'but the blessings always come more thickly than the troubles.'

'So you have found the silver lining to the cloud,' I said.

'That is it, ma'am; I have been a slow learner, but God has taught me at last, to trust Him in the dark, as well as in the light. I have found Him able to do exceeding abundantly above all that I can ask or think. His faithfulness reacheth unto the clouds. No words of mine can tell what He hath done for me,' she said.

'I do not wonder now, that your neighbours call you Heart's-ease,' I said, smiling.

'They seem to wonder why I am not worried, and fretted, and anxious as they are. Poor things! I wish they would try my way.'

'And what is your way?' I asked.

'It is to "cast all my care on Him who careth for me." When that is done, there is nothing left to worry about. How strange it is that people will keep their burdens and their worries, when they might so easily get rid of them! If we only trust God's promises, they will give us all the heart's ease that we need.'

And so we see, that it was the power of the promises which made that poor widow so happy and so useful. And if we make a right use of them, they will do the same for us.

I have just one other short story to illustrate the power of the promises. We may call it—

HEAVEN IN AN ALMSHOUSE.

A poor woman was dying, in the sick ward of a London Almshouse. A Christian lady, who was visiting there, came in to see her. As she entered the room, the dying woman exclaimed, 'What a precious Saviour Jesus is!'

'You know Him then, and love Him do you?' asked the visitor.

'Yes, I know Him, and love Him: His presence makes a heaven of this poor room. If you should heap up piles of gold and silver on my bed; if you could give me the queen's carriage and horses, her palace and garden, with health and strength to enjoy them all, I would not exchange for them my glorious Saviour, and the happiness I find in Him. They talk about the pains of dying; what will they be to me? They will only take me to Jesus, and to heaven.'

Certainly that poor woman was feeling the power of the promises. And so we see, that there are *three* good reasons, why these 'Bible Promises' may be spoken of as 'exceeding great and precious.'

They are so, in the first place, because of their *number;* in the second place, because of their *certainty;* and in the third place, because of their *power.*

The Collect for the Second Sunday in Advent, is a suitable one with which to close this sermon:—

'Blessed Lord, who hast caused all holy Scriptures to be written for our learning, grant that we may in such wise hear them, read, mark, learn, and inwardly digest them, that by patience and comfort of Thy holy word, we may embrace, and ever hold fast, the blessed hope of everlasting life, which Thou hast given us in our Saviour Jesus Christ. Amen.'

II.

THE PROMISE ABOUT PRAYER.

'*Ask, and it shall be given you.*'—St. Matt. vii. 7.

This is one of God's precious promises about prayer. There are a great many promises on this subject in the Bible. And we need them all. Every good thing that we hope for, either in this world, or in the world to come, we receive in answer to prayer. It is very important, therefore, for us to be sure, as the hymn says, that 'praying breath is never spent in vain.' There is nothing about which we need to be more certain than about *this*, that God *does* hear and answer prayer. And this is just what we are taught by our Saviour, when He says in the words of the text, 'Ask, and it shall be given you.' But does this mean that God will answer every prayer that we offer, no matter what we ask for? No; not by any means. When we ask God for anything, we must always ask for it in submission to His will. Our Saviour taught us this lesson by His own example. See, there He is in the garden of Gethsemane, just before His crucifixion. Bowed down to the earth, under the load of anguish that presses upon Him, He is engaged in earnest prayer. He has a full view of the awful sufferings of the cross, on which He is so soon to be nailed. His innocent nature shrinks from that terrible experience; and He offers this prayer: 'Father, if it be possible, let *this cup* pass from me!' The meaning of this was, 'Save me from being nailed to the cross!' But then He adds immediately, 'Nevertheless, not *My* will, but Thine be done.' He would ask for nothing that was contrary to His Father's will. And this is the example that we should follow. When we ask God to give us anything, we should always add—'if it be Thy will.' If any prayer could be answered contrary to the will of God, it would be sure to do us more harm than good.

There are only *three* kind of things that God promises to give to His people. And when we ask anything from Him, we should be sure that it is one of these three.

The first of these is—NECESSARY—*things.*

Suppose I should ask God to give me two heads, instead of one; would He answer that prayer? No. Why not? Because it is not necessary. Suppose I should ask God to give me wings like the eagle; would He answer that prayer? No. Why not? Because it is not necessary. Suppose I should ask God to give me one eye like a telescope, so that I could see the distant stars; and the other eye like a microscope, so that I could see those tiny things that cannot be seen without such a glass; would He answer that prayer? No. Why not? Because it is not necessary. Suppose I should ask God to give me two millions of pounds; would He answer that prayer? No. Why not? Because it is not necessary.

But on the other hand, suppose when I awake in the morning, that I ask God to give me help and strength, to serve Him faithfully all the day; will He answer that prayer? Yes. Why? Because *that is* necessary. Suppose that, before I lie down at night, I ask God to guard and keep me safely while I sleep; will He answer that prayer? Yes. Why? Because it is necessary; as I cannot take care of myself. And so, when we ask for necessary things, we may be sure they will be given, and the promise of the text be fulfilled.

And now let us look at some illustrations of the way in which God answers the prayers of His people for necessary things. Our first story may be called—

THE INDIAN'S PRAYER.

A young Chippewa Indian chief had become a Christian, and was successfully engaged in farming. In writing to the clergyman in New York, after whom he had been named at his baptism, he told him, with great pleasure, how well he was prospering in his new pursuit of farming; how many acres of land he had under cultivation—how many bushels of wheat, oats, and potatoes he had raised during the past summer—and how many oxen, cows, and hogs he had. 'All this,' said he, 'is wealth to me, beyond anything I ever dreamed of when I was a wild Indian. Then I had nothing, and never expected to have anything. I never asked God to make me rich; I only asked Him to forgive my sins. He answered that prayer, and then He gave me all the other good things, which I had not asked for.'

And God often does this. You remember what He did for Solomon. When he was first made king, God appeared to him in a dream, and told him to ask for anything he would like to have, and it should be given to him. Solomon asked God to give him wisdom, so that he might know how to govern his people, in the best possible way. This was a necessary thing that Solomon asked for. And God was so pleased with him, because he only asked for wisdom, that He promised not only to give him this, but also riches, and honour, and all other things that kings like to have. Our next story shows us how—

PRAYER FOR A BIBLE

was answered.

A colporteur, of the American Bible Society, was going through one of the countries in the State of Georgia, some time ago, selling Bibles and Testaments, and giving them away to those who were too poor to buy them. 'As I went on my way,' he says, 'I stopped one day at a small log house, on the road side, near some woods. The mother of the family living there bought a small Bible. Before I left she said to me: "I wish, my friend, you would go a little way into these woods. You will find a little cabin there. A good old widow woman lives in that cabin. She has no Bible, but wants one very much, though she is not able to buy one. But if you have any to give away, I am sure it will be a great comfort to her to have one."

'I walked a little way into the woods,' says the Bible man, 'and soon reached the little cabin. As I came near the door, I heard some one speaking. On listening, I soon found that it was the voice of prayer. The old widow was talking to God, and asking something from Him. I waited till she was through. Then I knocked at the door. She opened it herself, and received me with a pleasant smile.

I said to her, "My friend! I understand that you are in want of a Bible, and I have come on purpose to give you one." At the same time I offered her a copy of the Word of God. She took it eagerly in her hand, clasped it to her bosom, and then kissed it reverently, saying, as tears of gratitude ran down her cheeks: "This comes directly from the Lord. My minister has just been here to see me. He wanted to read the Bible to me; but I had none for him to use. This made me feel very badly. I said to myself, 'I must have a Bible; but I can't afford to buy one. What shall I do?' Then the thought came into my mind, I'll ask the Lord to give me one. So, when the minister left, I kneeled down, and told the Lord what I wanted, and asked Him to be so good as to send me one. I was praying for this when you came to the door. The promise is—'Ask, and it shall be given you.' The Lord knew it was necessary for me to have one, and so He has kindly sent it to me, just while I was asking for it. Oh, how good the Lord is!"'

I have one other story to illustrate this part of our subject. We may call it—

THE LITTLE BOY'S LETTER.

An officer, in the Russian army, died suddenly at Petersburg, leaving a wife and three small children, without any means of support. In a little while all their furniture, and clothing, had gone to the pawnbroker's, and there was no prospect before them but that of perishing from cold and hunger.

In their distress the oldest child, a little boy of six years old, thought that he must do something to help his mother and little sisters. In the first place, he went away by himself and prayed to God for help. Then he thought he would write a letter about it. So he wrote one, thus—

'DEAR LORD,—Mother and my two little sisters have nothing to eat, and are very hungry. Please send me a little money to buy them some bread, and when I get bigger, I will pay it back.

'Yours truly,

'* * * *'

He directed his letter to—'God in heaven.'

Then he went out, and ran to the nearest letter-box, to put his letter in. But he was too little to reach up to the opening in the box. There was a gentleman standing by, so he handed him the letter, and asked him to please drop it in the box. This gentleman happened to be the minister of a large church in that neighbourhood. When he saw what was written on the letter, he opened and read it. Then he went home with the little boy, and supplied the family, at once, with fuel and food. And on the next Sunday he told the story of the little boy to his congregation, and read them his letter. Then they took up a collection for the poor family. The collection amounted to fifteen hundred roubles, or about two hundred pounds of our money. The thing that little boy asked for was necessary, and it was given to him.

The first kind of things that God promises to give to those who ask is—necessary things.

The second kind of things that God will give us when we ask is—PROFITABLE—*things.*

There are many things which are not absolutely necessary for us, but which yet may be profitable. There, for example, is a drowning man. The most necessary thing in the world for him, is to have a rope thrown to him, that he may take hold of it, and be drawn out of the water. To a hungry man the thing most necessary is bread, to keep him from starving. To a sick man the necessary thing is medicine.

But here is a young man who just knows how to read, and write, and cypher. He wants very much to go to college, and get an education. That is not really necessary for him. He could live and be useful without it. But it would be very profitable for him. It would enable him to do many things, which he never could do without an education. And God promises to give us not only necessary things, but things that are profitable also. This is what He says: 'No *good* thing will He withhold,' from those who love and serve Him (Ps. lxxxiv. 11). The 'good things' here spoken of mean *profitable* things; or things that will help us in serving God, and trying to be more like Him. *We* do not know what things are profitable for us; but *God* knows. We sometimes ask for things which God sees it would not be good for us to have; and then He does not answer our prayers.

The Apostle Paul was troubled about something which he calls 'a thorn in the flesh.' He prayed to God three times to have it taken away. But his prayer was not answered. 'The thorn in the flesh' was not taken away; yet God promised to give him grace to bear it. He saw that it would be profitable to Paul to bear that thorn, and so He did not answer his prayer by taking it away. And thus, when we ask God to give us anything, we may be perfectly sure He will give it to us, if He sees that it will be for the good of our souls to have it. But if He sees that it will not be good, or profitable for us—then He will not give it to us.

Let us look at some examples of the way in which God answers His people's prayers, when they ask for profitable things. Our first story may be called—

THE WIDOW'S PRAYER ANSWERED.

A poor widow in Germany had two sons. She struggled hard to give them both a college education. Her youngest son was finishing his studies. The time for his last examination had come. After this was over he expected to get his diploma. That would cost fifty francs, or two pounds of our money. But his mother had not the money to pay for it. She was greatly distressed, because she knew not how to get it.

She went to see her minister about it. She told him of her trouble, and asked him what she was to do.

'You had better borrow the money,' he said.

'I cannot do that,' was her reply, 'for I know not how I can repay it.'

'Well,' said he, 'then let us ask God for the money. His promise is, "Call on Me in the day of trouble, and I will deliver thee" (Ps. l. 15). Go home and pray, and I will do the same in my study.' When she had gone, he knelt down, and engaged in earnest prayer for God to help her. He was too poor to give the money himself, and he wondered where it would come from.

Then he went to take a walk. In passing the house of a member of his church, it came into his mind to call and see them. As he entered the parlour the mother of the family said to him: 'You've come at the right time, we are very glad to see you, for we wish to ask your advice. Yesterday my husband and I celebrated our silver wedding. We have laid aside twenty-five florins, as a thank-offering to God, for all His goodness to us during the twenty-five years of our married life. But we know not what to do with it, and we wish you to tell us how to use it.'

The minister told them the story of the poor widow. They both exclaimed, 'It is the finger of God! Take the money and give it to her.'

He went directly to her house, and handing the money to her, told her how he got it. Tears of gratitude flowed down her cheeks as she clasped the money in her hand. Then they both kneeled down, and thanked God for His goodness in fulfilling His promise—'Ask, and it shall be given you.'

A florin is worth about eight shillings of our money; and so the twenty-five florins would be five times as much as the poor widow needed

Here is another illustration of the point of our subject now before us We may call it—

MONEY TO GO ON WITH.

A merchant in Liverpool, who was an earnest Christian man, met an acquaintance in the street one day. He knew he was living a very wicked life, and he thought he would speak a few words to him, with the hope of bringing him to the Saviour. But, just as he was beginning, his friend stopped him by saying: 'It's no use trying to make me a Christian. If I were one to-day, I should go back again to-morrow. You know how I'm living. But I've no power to break away from my bad habits, and do differently.'

'But suppose,' said his Christian friend, 'you should fail in business, as a merchant, and get into debt, what sort of a friend would you need to help you?'

'Why, I should want one who would pay my debts, and set me up in business again, and give me cash to go on with.'

'So you would,' said his friend. 'And this is just what Jesus will do for you. He not only pays our debts, but He sets us up again, and gives us the help of His grace; and *that* is the cash we need to go on with.'

This illustrates both points of the sermon we have had before us, and shows how God answers our prayers, for things that are necessary, and things that are profitable.

I have one other illustration of this part of our subject. We may call it—

CONNIE'S CHICKENS.

A little girl named Connie lived in the country. Not far from her home there was a large old barn. In this barn was an old hen, which belonged to Connie; and when this old hen hatched out seven little chickens, they belonged to Connie too.

One evening, just as Connie was going to bed, this barn caught fire. She saw the bright light flickering through the trees; and presently the great flames burst forth, all wrapped in clouds of smoke.

On seeing this Connie's little sister began to cry. She was about to do the same herself, when, all at once, a good thought came into her mind. So she turned away from the blazing barn, and kneeling down in a corner of the nursery, she offered this simple prayer: 'O God, please don't let my little chickens be burnt! Oh, don't let my little chickens be burnt, for Jesus' sake. Amen.'

The good Friend above, who gave the promise—'Ask, and it shall be given you,' heard that prayer for the little chickens, and answered it too. No one ever knew exactly how they got out of the barn; and of course the poor old hen could not tell about it. But the next morning, when Connie went out to look at the smouldering ruins of the barn, imagine her delight to see the old hen, clucking and scratching about, and her seven little chickens with her, all safe and sound. And if Jesus heard Connie's prayer, and saved her poor little chickens from the burning barn, we may be sure that He will hear us when we pray to be saved from that fire which will never be put out.

The second kind of things that God will give us when we ask, is—profitable things.

*And the third kind of things that God will give us, when we ask, is—*PROMISED*—things.*

If we ask for help to do any work we have to do, we shall be sure to get it, because God's promise is, 'I will help thee' (Is. xli. 10). If there are several things before us to attend to, and there is only one of them that can be done, and we know not which of them to choose, if we ask God to guide us in the matter, we may be sure that He will do it, because His promise is, 'In all thy ways acknowledge Me, and I will direct thy paths.' If we look to Jesus in faith, and ask Him to save our souls, we may be perfectly sure He will do it, for His promise is, 'Believe on the Lord Jesus Christ, and thou shalt be saved.' And it is just the same with all God's promises.

Balaam was speaking of the certainty of God's promises, when He asked the question: 'Hath He said, and shall He not do it? hath He spoken, and shall He not make it good?' When we take our stand on God's promises we are on ground that is perfectly sure. It never can fail us. When we ask for anything that God has promised, we never need have a moment's doubt about its being given to us. What God promises He never fails to perform. And so when we offer our prayers to God, and ask Him to give us anything, we must be sure that what we ask for is among the things He has promised; and then we may be sure that our prayers will be answered. Here are some incidents that illustrate this point very nicely. The first may be called—

HELP IN TROUBLE.

A brother of the Rev. Newman Hall, of London, was the superintendent of a Sunday school. One Saturday evening, the thought came into his mind that he ought to go and visit a certain member of the Bible-class connected with his school. He had never visited him before; but he felt that he must go now; and so he went. He found the young man very ill. His mother and sister were so well dressed, and everything about the house seemed so comfortable and respectable, that he felt unwilling to offer them any help. But he felt that he must do so; and at last he ventured to ask if there was anything he could do for them.

On hearing this, they both burst into tears and sobbed aloud. Then they told him that their patient had been asking for something to eat; but they had not a morsel of anything to give him, and not a penny left with which to buy a loaf of bread. 'We were asking God to help us, and just as you knocked at the door we were pleading that precious promise, in which God says, "Call on Me in the day of trouble, and I will hear thee." And it melts our hearts to find how wonderfully He fulfils His promises.'

The superintendent gave them what they needed then; and at once, by the help of a few friends, raised enough money effectually to relieve their wants. So the promise was fulfilled which says, 'Ask, and it shall be given you.'

The next story may be called—

WHAT GOD DOES WITH OUR SINS.

A little boy was once puzzled, when he heard two Christians talking about God's promise to 'blot out' His people's sins.

When he came home, he said, 'Mother, what becomes of all our sins when God forgives them?'

'Why, Charlie,' said his mother, 'can you tell me where all the figures are that you wrote on your slate yesterday?'

'I washed them all out, mother.'

'And where are they now?'

'Why, they are nowhere; they are put away—they are gone,' said Charlie.

'And that is just what God does with our sins,' said

his mother, 'when we repent, and believe in Jesus. God's promise is that they shall "be blotted out;" "they shall be *put away;*" they shall be "remembered no more;" "as far as the east is from the west, so far will He remove our trangressions from us." And when, in true penitence and faith, we ask Him to forgive us, and blot out our sins, we may be perfectly sure that what we ask for will be given us.'

Here is a nice little story, which may be called—

HE SAYS HE WILL.

A little child who had just lost her mother was asked one day, 'What do you do without a mother to tell your troubles to?'

She simply said, in answer to this question, 'I go to the Lord Jesus, and tell Him all my troubles; He was my mother's friend, and He's mine.'

'But Jesus is in heaven; there He sits on the throne of God. He has all the world to attend to, and a great many more worlds than this; and how do you think He can find time to attend to a poor little creature such as you are?'

'All I know about it is He says He will,' said the dear child, 'and that is enough for me.'

What a beautiful answer that was! That little girl was resting on God's promises, and she found great comfort in doing so. And if we learn to follow her example, it will make us happy.

I have just one other illustration. We may call it—

NETTIE'S DAILY BREAD.

A little girl, whose name was Nettie, lived with her mother in a small garret-room. One time her mother was sick; and they had no bread to eat. She was reading the thirty-third chapter of Isaiah that morning. In the sixteenth verse of this chapter, she found this sweet promise: 'Bread shall be given him, and his water shall be sure.' Then she kneeled down and said the Lord's Prayer. One clause in it she repeated several times: 'Give us this day our daily bread.' Then she went out into the street, and began to wonder where God kept His bread. She turned round the corner, and saw a large well-filled baker's shop.

'This,' said Nettie to herself, 'must be the place.' So she entered confidently and said to the big baker, 'I've come for it.'

'Come for what?'

'My daily bread,' said Nettie, pointing to the temping loaves. 'I'll take two, if you please—one for mother, and one for myself.'

'All right,' said the baker, putting them in a paper bag, and giving them to his little customer, who started at once for the door.

'Stop, you little rogue!' he said roughly; 'where is your money?'

The hard words frightened the poor child, and bursting into tears, she said: 'Mother is sick, and I am so hungry. I read in my Bible this morning God's promise which says, "Bread shall be given thee, and thy water shall be sure." Then in my prayer I said, "Give us this day our daily bread." Then I thought God meant me to come and fetch it; and so I came.'

The rough, but kind-hearted baker, was softened by the child's simple tale, and he sent her home not with two loaves merely, but with a well-filled basket.

Nettie was asking for what God had promised to give. Her prayer was answered, and she got what she asked for. And, if we follow her example, we shall find that the same God, who answered her prayer, will be ready to answer ours also; for His promise is—'Ask, and it shall be given you.'

Now where is our text to-day? St. Matthew vii. 7. What are the words of the text? 'Ask, and it shall be given you.'

What is the sermon about? God's promise to answer prayer. How many kind of things may we expect God to give us in answer to our prayers? Three. The first is what? *Necessary* things. The second is what? *Profitable* things. The third is what? *Promised* things.

So let us be careful in our prayers, to ask only for necessary, or profitable, or promised things; and then it will be our comfort to find, that the things which we ask for will surely be given unto us.

The Collect for the Tenth Sunday after Trinity is an appropriate one with which to close our sermon:—

'Let Thy merciful ears, O Lord, be open to the prayers of Thy humble servants; and that they may obtain their petitions, make them to ask such things as shall please Thee; through Jesus Christ our Lord. Amen.'

III.

THE BLESSING PROMISED IN CHRIST.

'*Men shall be blessed in Him.*'—Ps. lxxii. 17.

CHRISTMAS is the happiest season of the year. We generally receive presents from our friends at this time, and this is always pleasant. But there is *one gift*, which, more than any other, has to do with the happiness of Christmas. I refer here to God's great gift to our world. Jesus Himself said, 'God so loved the world, that He gave His only begotten Son, that whosoever believeth in Him should not perish, but have everlasting life.' And Christmas brings up afresh to our minds the thought of this great gift. We keep this happy season in memory of the time when Jesus was born. And the birth of Jesus was the greatest blessing that our world ever received. David was looking forward to the birth of Jesus when he said, 'Men shall be blessed in Him.'

And when we think of the different ways in which Jesus came to bless men, we see reason enough why we should be happy when Christmas comes. We shall only speak of *three* ways, in which men are blessed in Jesus.

In the first place Jesus blesses men by—THE KNOWLEDGE—*which He gives them.*

All the knowledge we have, of the world we live in, Jesus has given us. All the knowledge we have about ourselves; about our creation, and how we became sinful; about what we were sent into the world for; all we know about heaven—and how we are to pass through the world so as to get there safe at last: all this knowledge we owe to Jesus. It is the blessed Bible which tells us all we know about these things. But then we owe the Bible to Jesus. It was He who caused the Bible to be written; and He has told us everything that it contains. And when we think of the knowledge which the Bible gives us, on everything connected with our souls, and their salvation, and how we owe all this to Jesus; then we see how well it may be said—that 'men are blessed in Him.'

Let us look at some illustrations of the truth that men are blessed in Jesus, by the knowledge which He gives them.

Our first story may be called—

THE TARTAR CHIEFS.

Some years ago, two Tartar chiefs came from the borders of China to St. Petersburg, in Russia, to learn the language of that country, and some of the arts and customs of the Europeans. They brought letters with them, stating that they were two of the best men of their tribe.

A German missionary, who was translating a part of the New Testament into their native language, engaged them to help him in his work. They were occupied thus for several months. As they went on with their work from day to day, they often asked the missionary questions about Jesus the Saviour, and the truths which He taught.

When the translation was finished, the two chiefs sat in silence by the missionary, as if they were not willing to leave him. 'Have you any questions to ask, my friends?' said the missionary. 'None,' was their answer; 'but we wish to tell you that we are converted to the religion of that book'—pointing to the New Testament which lay on the table. 'We have lived in ignorance, and been led by blind guides. We have read the books which tell about the religion of the god Foh, who is worshipped in our country. But the more we read those books, the less we understood them, and the more empty our hearts remained. But in reading what that book tells us about Jesus, it is very different. The more we read the words of Jesus, the better we understand them. It seems as if Jesus Himself were talking to us. Now we know how to get our sins pardoned, and where to find the help we need, in trying to serve Him. That book satisfies our hearts, and makes us feel happy.'

Surely those men were blessed in the knowledge which Jesus gave them by His word!

Our next story may be called—

THE GOOD ONE BIBLE DID.

A Roman Catholic lady had been for some time in bad health, and very low spirits. One day, in walking through the streets of London, she passed by a theatre. Seeing the door open, and people going in, she supposed that some play was being performed, and concluded to go in and see it. But she had only been seated a few minutes when she heard some one say, 'Let us pray.' It seemed that a city missionary had hired the building for the purpose of holding a religious service in it, and was engaged in carrying it on. When the lady saw the mistake she had made, she rose to go out; but in doing this, she dropped her fan and her umbrella. The falling of these on the floor made so much noise, that every one turned and looked at her. Then she thought it best to sit down again, and listen to the minister. The words she heard had a strange effect upon her. She saw that she was a sinner, without any proper knowledge of the Saviour.

When the service was over she went up to the minister, and said she wished to speak with him. She told him of the burden of sin that was pressing upon her, and from which she had never found any relief.

'Oh! I have a cure for you. Take this book, and read it,' he said, as he handed her his pocket Bible. 'I am sure it will show you what to do with your sins, and make you feel happy.'

She took the book and promised to read it. She did so, and the reading of it made a great change in her. It led her to know and love the Saviour, as she had never done before. The burden of her sins was taken away, and this made her very happy.

Then she gave up going to the Romish Church. Before long the priest, who was a warm friend of hers, came to see her, and find out what was the matter. She showed him the book she had been reading, and told him what a wonderful change it had made in her views and feelings. 'I never knew what religion was before,' she said; 'but now, I am as happy as the day is long.'

Then she gave the book to him, and asked him to read it, and tell her what he thought of it.

The priest took the book and read it. The reading of it led to a change in him, like that which had taken place in his friend. But just after this he was taken very ill. This illness was followed by a sudden death. But the knowledge of Jesus, which the reading of that book had given him, took away all fear of death, and he died very happy.

During his sickness one of the nuns waited on him as a nurse. He told her about this book, and how much he had learned from it; and he asked her to have it put by his side in his coffin, to be buried with him. When he was placed in his coffin, the nun laid the Bible by his side. But, after thinking of the strange effect the reading of that book had produced on her friend the dead priest, she could not resist the strong desire that was in her heart to read it herself, and find out what was in it. And so, just before the lid of the coffin was fastened down, she took the book out of the coffin, and carried it to her own room, that she might have an opportunity, at her leisure, of reading it for herself. She did read it very carefully, and it had the same effect on her that it had on the priest and the lady. It taught her the truth in Jesus, as she had never known it before, and made her a happy and useful Christian.

Now surely it might well be said, of these three persons, that they were blessed in Jesus. Through the knowledge of Him, and His salvation, which they got from the simple reading of His word—they were 'blessed in Him.' The first way in which Jesus blesses men, is by the knowledge He gives them.

The second way in which men are blessed in Jesus, is by —THE PRIVILEGES—*which He bestows on them.*

It is a privilege to be the friend of any person who is good and great. Suppose that General Washington was living now, and was the president of the United States, what an honour it would be if you and I could be known as—*the friends of Washington.* But there is an honour greater even than this. When the patriarch Abraham was on earth, he was called '*the friend of God.*' What a privilege *that* was! And yet, if we only learn to love and serve Jesus, He will make this privilege ours. When He was on earth, He said to His disciples, 'Ye are *My friends.'* This is the greatest privilege that any one can have. I would rather be the friend of Jesus, though I had to live in a garret or a cellar, than to sit on the throne and wear the crown of the mightiest monarch on earth. And when we think of Jesus as making all His people His friends—the friends of God—how well it may be said that they 'are blessed in Him!'

Here is an illustration of the privilege of this friendship. We may call it—

THE BEST COMPANY.

One evening a lady who lived in New York was crossing the East River, in the ferry-boat, alone. As the boat drew near the landing, a bad man came up to her and said, 'Are you alone?'

'No, sir,' was her reply; and the moment the boat touched the wharf she jumped off.

Coming up to her again, as she was hurrying from the boat, the man said,—

'I thought you were alone.'

'I am not,' replied the lady.

'Why, I don't see any one; pray who is with you?'

'The Lord Almighty and the angels are my friends and companions. I am never alone,' was her answer.

'The company you keep, madam, is too good for me,' said the man, and then he went off. Now certainly that good lady was feeling that it was a privilege to have the friendship of God.

And the *protection* of God, as well as His friendship, is one of the privileges that Jesus secures for His people. If we could draw a line around our dwelling, and then arrange things so that no one could ever cross that line to do us harm, what a privilege that would be! We cannot do this for ourselves; but this is just what Jesus does for His people.

When Job was on earth, Satan tried hard to do him some harm. But he found it impossible to touch a hair of his head. And he said the reason of it was, that God had 'made a hedge about him, and about his house, and about all that he had on every side.' Satan had tried to leap over that hedge, or to force his way through it. But it was impossible. He never could do it till God gave him leave. Job was enjoying the privilege of God's protection, that we are now speaking of. And God puts the same sort of a hedge about all His people that He put around Job. And it is a very great privilege to have such protection.

The Bible tells us that God 'holds His people in the hollow of His hand;' 'He keeps them as the apple of His eye;' He 'puts underneath them His everlasting arms;' and spreads over them His sheltering wings: then, how safe they are! And if we are God's people, though all the wicked men and all the evil spirits in the world should try to injure us, they never could do it. We are perfectly safe under God's protection. What a privilege this is!

Let us look at one or two illustrations of this privilege. The first we may call—

THE ANGEL'S CHARGE.

Annie was a timid little girl. She did not like to be left alone in a dark room. One night when she had said her prayers, her mother helped her into bed, and giving her a good-night kiss, was just leaving the room when she heard Annie say very softly, 'Mamma!'

She went back to her little girl's bedside, to see what she wanted. Finding that she was frightened by the rattling of the windows as the wind blew against them, her mother put some wedges in the windows to stop their rattling. And then, sitting down by little Annie's bed, she said,—

'You don't feel afraid now, darling, when I am with you, do you?'

'Oh no, mamma! I don't mind the noise, or feel afraid of anything, when you are here.'

'And yet, Annie dear, your Heavenly Father can take much better care of you than I can; and He is with you all the time. Let me teach you a beautiful verse from the Bible, which I wish you to remember, and repeat to yourself, whenever you feel afraid. It is this "He shall give His angels charge over thee, to keep thee in all thy ways. They shall bear thee up in their hands, lest thou dash thy foot against a stone." And now I want my little girl to say this verse over till she knows it and can remember it as long as she lives.'

Annie repeated it several times, and then she said, 'Now, mamma, you may go down-stairs. I'll not be afraid any more.'

So her mamma kissed her, and went away; and little Annie closed her eyes, and went to sleep, saying, 'God's angels will take care of me' (Ps. xxxiv. 7).

Here is another nice story, to illustrate this part of our subject. We may call it—

THE STORM AND ITS LESSONS.

A severe thunderstorm was raging one night. Two little girls had been put early to bed that evening. The flashing of the lightning, and the rolling of the thunder, frightened the children, so that trembling they hid their faces beneath the bed-clothes.

A young house-maid was passing backwards and forwards in the entry, outside their room, attending to her duties. While thus engaged, the children heard her singing, with her sweet young voice, these words of one of her favourite hymns :—

> 'O God, our help in ages past,
> Our hope for years to come ;
> Our shelter from the stormy blast,
> And our eternal home !
>
> 'Under the shadow of Thy throne,
> Thy saints have dwelt secure ;
> Sufficient is Thine arm alone,
> And our defence is sure.'

'Jane, Jane,' cried one of the children from the bedroom, 'aren't you afraid? 'How can you keep on singing, when it lightens so, and the thunder makes such a dreadful noise?'

'Afraid, Miss Annie? Oh no,' said the girl. 'How can I be afraid when I know that God is here? He takes care of me, and nothing can hurt me without His will. The lightning can do nothing but what God sends it to do. So don't be afraid; but just try to think that *you must be safe in God's keeping.* He will take care of both you and me.'

Then Jane kissed the children, and bade them 'good-night.' Her words comforted them, and took away their fear, and they fell asleep thinking of these sweet words: 'God will take care of us.'

When we think of the privileges which Jesus bestows upon His people, of His friendship, and protection, we see how well it may be said, that 'men shall be blessed in Him.' *And in the third place, men are blessed in Jesus by*—THE HOPE—*He imparts to them.*

A heart without any hope, is like a lantern that has no light in it. And yet, until we learn to know and love

Jesus, we never can have any hope of pardon, or of heaven. This hope, which Jesus gives, is one of the greatest blessings that we can have. What a dark and dreary place this world would be to live in, if we had no sun to shine upon us! And as the sun by his bright beams lights up the world around us, so Jesus lights up the hearts of His people, and fills them with joy and gladness, by the hope of heaven which He gives them.

Suppose that you and I were visiting a hospital. In one ward we find men suffering from broken limbs; in another they are sick with fever; and in another with consumption. One ward is full of men who are blind, and another with those who are deaf. And suppose that none of them have any hope of getting well, or ever being any better. How sad and sorrowful they would all be! But suppose that, as we walked through the wards of that hospital, we were able to give to all those poor sufferers the sure hope that, in a short time, they would all get quite well,—the blind eyes would be opened; the deaf ears would be unstopped; the broken limbs would all be healed; those suffering from consumption and fever would be cured; and all would go out of the hospital, in good health and strength;—what a change our visit would make to those poor suffering patients! And how well it might have been said that they were blessed in us! We had blessed them by the hope of getting well, which we had given them. And it is just so, that men are blessed in Jesus. Sin has made our world like a great hospital, all the wards of which are full of people suffering from different kinds of disease. In themselves they have no hope of ever being any better. But Jesus gives the sure hope of getting well, to all who love and serve Him. And so it is true that 'men are blessed in Him,' by the hope He gives them of having their sins pardoned, and of going to heaven by and by. Here are some illustrations of the way in which men are blessed by the hope which Jesus gives. The first we may call—

THE MINER'S BOY AND HIS BIBLE.

A poor coal miner, who feared God, was in the habit of always taking his Bible with him when he went down into the pit, that he might read a few verses when he left off work to eat his dinner. He had a son, a little lad, who worked with him. He had received a Bible from his Sunday-school teacher, and by the advice of his father he was in the habit of taking it with him too.

One day, while they were at work, there was an accident in the mine. A great mass of coal, forming the roof above them, fell to the earth, between the father and the son. The father was not hurt, but he was in great distress to know how it was with his son. He called aloud to him. The boy answered him; but it was only to say, that his feet were both crushed under heavy pieces of coal, and he could not move. 'What can I do for you, my poor dear boy?' exclaimed the father.

'Nothing, I fear,' said the boy; 'but my lamp is not out yet. I am reading my Bible with great comfort; and I feel that the Lord is with me.'

Help was called for, and after some hours of hard labour, the boy was reached. But he was found dead. His lamp had gone out: but the lamp of life—his blessed Bible—had kindled the hope of heaven in his soul. He was blessed in Jesus, by the hope which He gives His people. And what else was there, in all the world, which could have cheered and comforted that dear boy when he had to meet death, all alone amidst the deep darkness of that gloomy pit?

We have a beautiful hymn in our hymnal, the first line of which reads thus—

'Abide with me, fast falls the even-tide.'

This hymn was written by an English clergyman. He wrote another very precious hymn, on the words—'I am Christ's and Christ is mine.' I will quote several verses of this hymn, because it illustrates the point of our subject now before us, showing how Jesus blesses men by the glorious hope which He puts in their hearts. Listen to these verses—

'The good I have is from His stores supplied;
The ill is only what He deems the best;
If He's my friend, I'm rich with naught beside,
And poor without Him, though of all possessed:
Changes may come; I take, or I resign;
Content while I am His, and He is mine.

'Whate'er may change, in Him no change is seen;
A glorious sun, that wanes not, nor declines;
Above the clouds and storms, He walks serene,
And sweetly on His people's darkness shines:
All may depart, I fret not, nor repine,
While I my Saviour's am, and He is mine.

'He stays me falling, lifts me up when down;
Reclaims me wandering, guards from every foe;
Plants on my worthless brow the victor's crown,
Which in return before His feet I throw,—
Grieved that I cannot better grace His shrine,
Who deigns to own me His, as He is mine.

'While here, alas! I know but half His love,
But half discern Him, and but half adore;
But, when I meet Him in the realms above,
I hope to love Him better, praise Him more;
And feel, and tell, amid the choir divine,
How fully I am His, and He is mine.'

Here is a good illustration of this part of our sermon. We may call it—

GLORIOUS DYING.

There were two brothers who were very much attached to each other. The elder was named George, and the younger Charles. Whatever George did, Charles always wanted to do too. During the war, George came home one day, and said he had just enlisted in the army. Then Charles said he must enlist too. So he went to the recruiting officer, and got his name entered next to his brother's.

'George and I,' he said to the officer, 'have never been separated for a day, all our lives, and I must go with him into the army.'

So they went, and were in a number of battles together, without being wounded.

But in the terrible battle of Perryville, George was mortally wounded. A minie ball had passed through his lungs. As soon as Charles saw his brother fall, he went up to him, and kneeling by his side, put his knapsack under his head for a pillow, and made him as comfortable as he could. Then he kissed him, and was going away when George said to him,—

'Wait a little, Charley. Stoop down and let me give you my last kiss.' George gave him a kiss for himself. Then he gave him another, and said, 'Now, Charley, I want you to take that kiss home to mother, and tell her that I died praying for her.'

Charley stood there gazing at his brother, as he lay before him, bleeding to death. While he was looking at him he heard George say, 'This is glorious!'

'What is glorious, brother?' said Charley. 'I don't see anything very glorious, for you to be lying here, weltering in your blood.'

'Oh yes, Charley,' said George, 'it is glorious to be looking up to heaven, as I am doing, and to see Jesus waiting to receive me.'

That poor dying soldier was blest in Jesus, by the hope of heaven which He gave him.

Here are some simple lines with which we may finish our sermon. They are called *The Song of Hope.* They show us how hope sheds its cheering light along the pathway of our pilgrimage:—

'I hear it singing, singing sweetly,
Softly in an undertone,
Singing as if God had taught it,
"It is better farther on."

'Night and day it sings the song,
Sings it while I sit alone,
Sings so that the heart may hear it,
"It is better farther on."

'Sits upon the grave and sings it,
Sings it when the heart would groan,
Sings it when the shadows darken,
"It is better farther on."

'Farther on? How much farther?
Count the milestones one by one;
No! no counting—only trusting,
"It is better farther on."'

Where is our text? Ps. lxxii. 17. What are the words of the text? 'Men shall be blessed in Him.' What is the sermon about? How men are blessed in Jesus. How many ways did we speak of? Three. In the first place Jesus blessed His people by what? By *the knowledge* He gives. In the second place by what? By *the privileges* He bestows on them. And in the third place by what? By *the hope* He imparts to them.

The Collect for the Sixth Sunday after the Epiphany is a very appropriate one with which to close this sermon:—

'O God, whose blessed Son was manifested that He might destroy the works of the devil, and make us the sons of God, and heirs of eternal life; Grant us, we beseech thee, that having this hope, we may purify ourselves, even as He is pure; that when He shall appear again, with power and great glory, we may be made like unto Him in His eternal and glorious kingdom; where with Thee, O Father, and Thee, O Holy Ghost, He liveth and reigneth, ever one God, world without end. Amen.'

IV.

THE PROMISED HELP.

'I will help thee.'—ISA. xli. 10.

SOME years ago, a gentleman said to me one day, 'Dr. Newton, will you please tell me what verse of the Bible has been the greatest use and comfort to you, in all the years of your Christian life?'

Without a moment's hesitation, I said, in answer to his question, 'Why, sir, the four central words in the tenth verse of the forty-first chapter of Isaiah: "*I will help thee.*"' These words have been the staff of my pilgrimage, for more than half a century. When I have had any hard work to do, or any heavy burden to bear, I have always leaned on this staff, and have been helped and strengthened by it. It has never broken, and never bent under me when I have leaned upon it; but has been a comfort and support to me, times and ways without number.'

This is one of the most precious of the 'Bible Promises.' And so, in speaking about it, we may well say that our sermon to-day is about *the promised help.* God says to each of His people—'I will help thee.'

And there are three things we have to do, in each of which we especially need the help thus promised.

In the first place we need this help—IN RESISTING OUR TEMPTATIONS.

Satan is the great tempter. This is his special business. But he does not work alone, in carrying on this business. He has a multitude of evil spirits—fallen creatures like himself—to assist him. And then he makes use of wicked men, as well as evil spirits, to help him in this work. All these taken together are like a great army of tempters, and Satan is the leader, or general, of this army. They are busy all the time, in laying temptations along the paths in which we have to walk every day. But if we are left to ourselves, if we do not have the help which God promises us, we could no more resist these temptations than an infant could break away from the grasp of a mighty giant.

When Joseph was in the house of Potiphar, he was tempted to commit a great sin. But God helped him to remember that *He* was present with him, and looking at him. And this thought gave him power to resist the temptation. Joseph said to his tempter, 'How can I do this great wickedness, and sin against God?' If we could always remember these four words,—'*Thou God seest me,*' —it would be a great help to us in resisting temptation.

One day, when Jesus was on earth, he saw that Satan was preparing a very dangerous temptation for the Apostle Peter. By means of this temptation Satan expected to prevent Peter from ever becoming a preacher of the gospel, and to cause the loss of his soul. And no doubt this result would have followed, if Jesus had not helped Peter at the time of that temptation. But He said to him, 'I have prayed for thee, that thy faith fail not.' That prayer of Jesus was the only thing that helped Peter then, and kept him from being entirely lost through that temptation.

Here are some illustrations of the ways in which God helps His people to resist temptation. The first may be called—

TEMPTATION TO DRINK OVERCOME BY PRAYER.

There was a poor man living in a town near Boston, who had become a confirmed drunkard. His friends made every effort to save him, but in vain. He resolved again and again to break away from the temptation to drink, but he could not. He made the most solemn vows to reform, but Satan was too strong for him. He lost his situation, and could get no work.

Then he concluded to go to Cape Cod, and try to get employment in fishing. Here he became acquainted with a young man who had been a fisherman all his days. 'He was very kind to me,' said this man in speaking of it afterwards. 'He had a remarkably pleasant face, and was always ready to show me any favour. One day I was so touched by his many kindnesses, that I pulled out my flask of liquor and offered him a drink.'

'"No," said he, "I never taste intoxicating liquor, and I have asked the Lord Jesus to help me never to touch it."

'I looked at him with surprise.

'"Are you a Christian?" I asked.

'"Yes,"' said he.

'"And does Jesus keep you from using intoxicating drink?"

'"He does," said he, "and I have no desire to touch it."

'This answer set me to thinking. It showed me a new help; one that I had never tried. On my way home that night, I said to myself, "How do I know but that Jesus would help me to quit drinking, if I should ask Him?" As soon as I got to my room, I knelt down and told the Lord Jesus what a miserable wretch I was; how long I had fought against my appetite for strong drink, but had always been overcome. I told Him that if He would help me to resist the temptation to drink, I would give myself up to Him for ever, and love and serve Him all my days. Jesus heard and answered my prayer. He took away my love for strong drink. From that blessed hour, I have never tasted a drop of intoxicating liquor, and have no desire to do so. When I gave myself to Jesus I felt that I received help from Him, against every enemy of my salvation.'

Certainly the promise of the text was fulfilled in that man's experience.

Our next story will show—

HOW THE TEMPTATION TO BREAK THE SABBATH WAS RESISTED.

Some years ago, it happened that the Prince of Wales, who was afterwards George IV., king of England, sent for a tradesman, whom he often employed, to attend to some business for him on Sunday, as he was preparing to leave town the next day. This tradesman was an earnest Christian man, and one who had great regard for the Lord's day. The favour and patronage of the Prince of Wales were very valuable to him in his business, and he was very unwilling to think of offending him, and losing his support. Here was a great temptation for him to break the Sabbath. But, on the other hand, he knew it was contrary to the command of God for him to work on that day. And in a matter of this kind he felt that he must obey God rather than man. And this thought helped him to resist the temptation thus brought before him to break the Sabbath. He declined to answer the Prince's summons on God's holy day. But he took care to be at the palace very early the next morning.

'I sent for you yesterday,' said the Prince; 'why did you not come?'

'Please your Royal Highness, the King wanted me.'

'The king! why I thought my father never sent for his tradesmen on Sundays.'

'Please your Royal Highness, I do not mean the king your father, but God—the King of kings. He has told me that I must not work on Sundays. And, as I value my soul, I dare not disobey *His* command.

'That was right,' said the Prince. 'I have nothing more to say. I am very sure that the man who is faithful to his Master in heaven, will be true to his earthly master.'

Here we see how Jesus helped this man to resist the temptation to which he was exposed, of breaking the fourth commandment.

We have one other story on this point of our subject. We may call it—

A SCOTCHMAN'S STRUGGLE WITH TEMPTATION.

Striker Stowe was the head workman, in the large steel works at Glasgow. He held the position of 'boss striker' in those works. All the men in that establishment were hard drinkers. Stowe himself had been the same, for years.

One day it was announced among the workmen that Stowe had become a Christian, and had joined the church.

The next time one of the men asked him to drink, his reply was: 'No, my lads, I shall never drink any more intoxicating liquor. For the Bible says that—"no drunkard shall inherit the kingdom of God."'

The men smiled at each other when they heard this,

and said: 'Wait till hot weather comes. When he gets as dry as dust, he'll give in. He can't help it.'

But right through the hottest summer weather, Stowe worked away till the sweat was pouring off him in streams; yet he never touched a drop of liquor.

One day the superintendent of the works said to him: 'Well, Stowe, you used to drink a good deal of liquor. Don't you miss it?'

'Yes, I do.'

'But how do you manage to get on without it?'

'I'll tell you. See there's my almanac. From seven to eight o'clock, this morning, I asked the Lord to help me to resist this temptation to drink. He did so. Then I put a dot in my almanac. From eight to nine He helped me, and I put down another dot. Just as I put it down I prayed, "O Lord, help me another hour." So I go on through the day, and it keeps me full of peace and joy to think that the Lord is near, helping me all the time.'

Here we see how beautifully the promise of the text was fulfilled in this man's case, as the Lord helped him to resist temptation. The first way in which we need God's promised help is in resisting our temptations.

The second way in which we need this help is—IN BEARING OUR BURDENS.

We all have burdens to bear, of one kind or another, in this world. These burdens are made up of the cares and trials of life. Whether we are rich or poor; whether we are young or old; there is some burden for us to bear Job says that 'man is born unto trouble as the sparks fly upwards.' These troubles make up our burdens; and in bearing these burdens we need help. We are not able of ourselves to bear them. But there is one precious promise of the Bible that meets us, just here. It is that in which David says, 'Cast thy burden upon the Lord, and He shall sustain thee' (Ps. lv. 22). God can put His everlasting arms under us; and with the help which He thus gives, the heaviest burden will be light, and easy to bear. Many of the early Christians had all their possessions taken away from them when they became the followers of Jesus. This was a heavy burden for them to bear. Yet God gave them such help that they were able to 'take *joyfully* the spoiling of their goods.' At the time when the Apostle Paul became a Christian, he had the prospect of great honour and riches, in the path of life that was opening before him. But in connecting himself with the cause of Jesus, he had to let that prospect go. That was a heavy burden for him to bear. But the help he found in bearing it was so great, that he looked on the loss of all earthly things 'as a gain that he might win Christ.' And now let us look at some other illustrations of the way in which God helps His people in bearing their burdens. The first we may call—

THE ROPE AT SEA.

'When I made my first sea voyage,' said a minister of gospel, 'I had great difficulty in trying to stand upright. As soon as the weather became rough and stormy, I found myself staggering like a drunken man, and sometimes I would be thrown flat upon the deck. One day, after tossing about, on this side and that, I saw a good strong rope hanging down from the rigging. I took a firm hold of it; and oh, what a help it was to me! I didn't mind how rough the sea was; or how much the vessel tossed about. I could stand up comfortably, so long as I held on to that rope.'

Now our life in this world is like a voyage on the ocean. And, when storms of trouble overtake us, we often find it hard to stand upright. But God has given us the precious promises of His word, to be to us just what that rope was to the landsman, on his first voyage. If we take them one by one, and hold fast on to them, as he did to the rope, they will help us to bear our burdens; and to stand upright with comfort, no matter how hard the wind blows, or how much our vessel tosses about.

Our next illustration may be called—

COMFORT IN TROUBLE.

A good minister in England told his three children one day, that he was going to take them to see one of the most interesting sights they would ever meet with. Then he went out to walk with them, and led them to a poor, miserable hovel. The walls were crumbling to decay. The windows were broken, and everything about it told of poverty and want. 'Now, my dear children,' said the father, 'do you think that any one, living in such a wretched place as this, can be happy? But in this cottage is a poor young man. He lies on a bed of straw. He is dying with fever. He has nine large painful sores, in different parts of his body; and yet he is one of the happiest men I know of.' 'How can that be possible?' exclaimed the children. 'My children, that is just what I brought you here to see.' Then he led them into the cottage, and going up to the poor dying young man, he said, 'Abraham, my friend, I have brought my children here to see you. I wish them to learn that people can be happy in sickness, in poverty, in suffering and want; now tell them if it is not so.'

The suffering youth immediately answered, 'Oh! yes, sir, it is so. I would not exchange my state with the richest man in the country, if he did not know and love my precious Saviour. Sir, this sickness and these sores are nothing to me when God is present with me, filling my soul with peace and joy. I am indeed truly happy; and every hour of my life I thank God, for the riches of His grace and goodness to me, in Jesus Christ.'

What a beautiful illustration this is, of the way in which God helps His people to bear their burdens, no matter how heavy they be!

I have one other incident to illustrate this part of our subject. We may call it—

THE HEAVY BURDEN MADE LIGHT.

A Christian mother, named Mrs. Norton, had a little daughter born to her. Mrs. N. already had three sons, and she had long desired to have a daughter, and it was a day of gladness, not only to the mother, but to all the family, when this little girl was born. Her mother nursed her with the greatest interest and affection. For a while everything went on pleasantly in this family.

But at length, the mother began to feel very uneasy about her child. There was a great difference between her and the other children in their infancy. She never smiled, or took any notice of her mother, or the rest of the family. In her anxiety, Mrs. Norton consulted their family physician about it. He examined the little one very carefully. As he did so his face grew very sad, and finally, with his eyes full of tears, he said: 'My dear friend, I am very sorry for what I have now to tell you, but the fact is your child has no mind. She is an idiot.' What a blow that was to fall on a fond mother! How heavy a burden of sorrow was thus fastened upon her! At first she came near sinking, under the weight of this great affliction. But soon she got over this; and notwithstanding the trouble thus brought upon her, she always had a calm, cheerful, happy look.

The idiot child proved a blessing to her, and to the rest of the family.

One day a friend said to her: 'Mrs. Norton, how is it possible for you to be so happy and cheerful, when you have such a heavy burden of sorrow to bear? Will you please tell me the secret of it?'

'That I will gladly do,' said Mrs. Norton. 'This is the greatest affliction I ever had to bear. At first I thought it would break my heart. I never expected to have one happy feeling, as long as I lived. But, as I awoke from sleep one morning, soon after this trouble came upon me, I heard sounding in my ears, as a voice from heaven, the words which Pharaoh's daughter spoke to the mother of Moses, when she put in her care the child which had been taken from the ark of bulrushes, and said, "Take this child and nurse it for me, and I will give thee thy wages." I knew it was my Father in heaven who was speaking those precious words to me; and it made a wonderful change in my thoughts and feelings towards my poor child. It lightened my burden, and gave me all the help I have needed in bearing it. Since then I have never felt sad or sorrowful about this matter. I say to myself, "The child is God's. He knows what is best for is. All I have to do is to nurse it well;" and the thought that I am doing this for God, makes it a pleasure and delight to me. This is the secret of my being so cheerful and happy.'

How wonderfully God helped that Christian mother to bear her burden.

The second way in which we need God's help is in bearing our burdens.

The third way in which we need God's help is—IN DOING OUR DUTY.

Whether we are young or old we all have duties of one kind or another to attend to. At home, or at school, or at our place of business, wherever we go, there are some things which it is our duty to do. And we need help in doing these things. And it is just here that the precious promise of our text comes in. When our Saviour was on earth, He said to His disciples, 'Without Me ye can do nothing.' And what was true of them, is equally true of you, and me, and all of us. We need help in the daily duties that we have to attend to. And this is what God promises to give us, when He says in our text, 'I will help thee.' And if we only secure this promised help, we shall be able to get comfortably through with all our duties.

The Apostle Paul was rejoicing in this help, when he said, 'I can do all things through Christ strengthening me.' And what wonderful things St. Paul was able to do by the help or strength which he received from Jesus! Like Him he 'went about doing good.' He spent his life in making missionary journeys all over the earth. Where-ever he went, he was occupied in telling the story of Jesus and His love; and showing men what they must do to be saved. We cannot find a better illustration anywhere, of the way in which God helps His people to do their duty, than we have in the life and labours of this great apostle. And if we seek it from Him, God is ready to give us the same help that He gave to St. Paul. The promise of the text—'I will help thee'—was fulfilled in St. Paul's case, and it will be fulfilled in ours too, if we ask for it.

And now, let us look at some other illustrations of the way in which God gives His people the help here promised in doing their duty.

Our first illustration may be called—

HELP IN MAKING A SERMON.

The incident, now to be mentioned, occurred in my own experience.

Some years ago, at the close of one of the children's services, at the Church of the Epiphany, I found, on looking a month ahead, that our next service for the young would be on the afternoon of Easter day, and for that occasion a sermon on the resurrection would be necessary. I felt anxious about this; and so, on the evening of the next day—Monday—I went to my study, to try and lay out that sermon. The text chosen for that occasion was our Saviour's words to Mary: 'I am the resurrection.' I wrote down the text, and tried to arrange the outline of the sermon. But I could not start a single thought. Then I walked up and down my study, and tried, and tried again to open the subject, but in vain. I could not do anything with it. Then I kneeled down, and told the Lord about my trouble. I pleaded the promise of our text—'I will help thee.' I asked the Lord to fulfil His promise, once more, as He had often done before. Then I tried again to start my sermon, and kept on trying, till it was past ten o'clock; but I could do nothing with it. I gave it up for the night, and prepared for bed.

In doing this I said to myself: 'Well, the promised help has not come yet. But I am perfectly sure *it will come;* for it is God's promise, and that cannot fail.'

I rose early the next morning to go to church, as we had service at half-past eight. As I was walking up Chestnut Street, on my way to church, just as I got opposite to Mr. Baldwin's conservatory, next door to the American Sunday-School Union, I said to myself, 'Well, how about my sermon for the Easter day's service?' and then, just as quick as a flash, a beautiful and proper plan for that sermon came into my mind. How happy I felt! I went on my way rejoicing. As soon as the service at church was over, I hastened to my study, put down the plan of that sermon, and then went to work and wrote it out, just as it had been suggested to me.

Now, if the angel Gabriel had met me that morning in Chestnut Street; if he had handed me a roll, saying, as he did so—'This is the plan for that sermon on the resur rection, which the Lord wishes you to write;'—I should have known where that sermon came from. I saw no angel, and received no roll. But I am just as sure that my Father in heaven gave me the plan of that sermon, as though the angel had brought it to me. The promise of the text was fulfilled in my experience then. The Lord helped me to make that sermon.

I have only one other illustration to give of this subject. We may call it—

HOW A LITTLE BOY WAS HELPED TO DO HIS DUTY BOTH AT HOME AND AT SCHOOL.

Albert Collins had entered the primary department of the public school, and had been going there for several months. He had made up his mind always to be at school before the bell quit ringing in the morning, so as never to get a bad mark for being late.

But December had come, and the mornings were short; and there was a lively time in his mother's little home, because there were so many things to be done by nine o'clock, when the school bell stopped ringing.

One morning, Albert's mother asked him to mind the baby, while she went round the corner to get some yeast from their neighbour, Mrs. Brown. This was just a little while before school time. Mrs. Collins got talking with Mrs. Brown, and forgot all about Albert and the school.

The little fellow, with his over-shoes and scarf on, and his cap in his hand, stood by the cradle rocking it, but keeping his eye on the clock. Five minutes—ten minutes passed away—and there were only five minutes more before the bell would stop ringing—and he would get a bad mark for being late. He went to the door and looked towards the corner. But his mother was not in sight. Then he put his hand to his mouth, and shouted, as loud as he could, 'Mamma—come—home!' But there was no answer. Then he ran back to the cradle, saying, 'Oh, dear, dear, what shall I do? I cannot leave the darling baby, and yet, I do so want to get to school before the bell stops ringing!'

Then a happy thought came into his mind. He said to himself, 'I'll take the baby to school with me.' So he took the baby out of the cradle, wrapped an old shawl about her, and snatching her half-filled bottle of milk, he dashed out of the room, and ran towards the school as fast as his stout young legs would carry him. The baby was a little mite, only two months old, and Albert was nearly six, and large for his age.

Just after leaving the house he met two women whom he knew: 'Why, Albert?' said one of them, 'what on earth!—' but he bounded past, and reached the school just before the bell stopped ringing. He laid his funny burden down in the arms of his astonished teacher.

'I couldn't leave her at home,' he said, 'and I *couldn't* be late, so I brought her along. She'll go to sleep, and be real good.'

The teacher began to unwind the shawl. Then all the scholars saw a surprised, half-smothered looking little baby, still in her night-gown, with one bare foot sticking out, and her little fists tightly clenched, as if defying any one to take her home.

The teacher was a good-natured young lady, and, as she looked at this strange sight, she laughed till she almost dropped the baby on the floor. The whole school laughed with her. This brought the principal of the school in, from the next room, to see what was the matter. He was a grave, stern-looking man; and there was a frown upon his face as he entered the room. But no sooner did he see the strange looking tiny baby there, than the frown passed off, and he laughed too, as heartily as any of them.

While this was going on at school, Albert's mother had returned to her home. She went first to the cradle—but to her surprise and horror the baby was not there. Then she ran through the four rooms of her little home, but could see nothing of either of her children. The dreadful thought came into her mind, that they had been stolen, like poor little Charley Ross. This almost made her crazy. She put on her bonnet and shawl and hastened into the street. There, the first person she met was the woman who had spoken to Albert when he was hurrying to school. 'What's the matter, Mrs. Collins?' she asked. 'Oh, I don't know what's become of my children?' 'Why,' said the woman, 'I met Albert, a little while ago, kiting along like the wind, with the baby in his arms. Leastways I thought it was the baby from the way he carried it.'

'Is it possible that he has taken her to school?' Then she started, and ran for the school as fast as she could go. Arriving there, panting, and out of breath, she entered, and asked, 'Is—is—my—my baby here?'

The baby was handed to her, and wrapping her cloak around it, she thanked the teacher, and walked home feeling very happy.

At first Mrs. Collins felt angry with Albert for taking the baby to school; but when she remembered that it was done out of his desire not to be late and get a bad mark, her anger passed away, and she saw that she was to blame herself, for staying so long at Mrs. Brown's. And when she found that the baby was none the worse for her little runaway, she had to laugh over it too. And when Albert came home to dinner, she made an apology

'SHE MADE AN APOLOGY TO HIM FOR STAYING AWAY SO LONG.'

to him for staying away so long. Then he hugged her and kissed her, and said he was glad he 'didn't leave the baby, 'cause she might have been burned up; and he thanked God for helping him to do his duty, both at home and at school.'

We have spoken now of three ways, in which God fulfils the promise of the text, by helping His people.

In the first place, He helps us to resist our temptations; in the second place, He helps us to bear our burdens; and in the third place, He helps us to do our duty.

Let us always look to Him for help, and then we shall be able to resist our temptations—to bear our burdens—and to do our duty with glory to God, and with comfort to ourselves!

V.

THE PROMISE OF FINDING GOD.

'*Those who seek Me early shall find Me.*'—PROV. viii. 17.

THIS is one of God's precious promises for the young. It is intended to encourage us all to do what our Saviour was speaking of when He said, 'Seek ye—*first*—the kingdom of God, and His righteousness.'

There are many things we have to do in this world, which we cannot begin to do till we reach a certain age. Suppose, for instance, that one of the larger boys here present should make up his mind to be a minister, could he begin at once to preach? No; not at all. He might begin at once to study for the ministry. But he could not begin to preach till he was ordained; and he could not be ordained till he was about twenty-one years of age.

And so, if you wanted to be a physician, or a lawyer, or a merchant, or a mechanic,—you could not enter immediately on the duties of any of these pursuits. You would have to serve a sort of apprenticeship to the business on which you wished to enter, and wait till you had learned how to do it, before you could begin its duties.

But it is very different with the matter of seeking Jesus, or trying to be a Christian. For this, it is not necessary to wait any longer. The youngest child here present may begin at once to seek and to serve Jesus.

'When little Samuel woke,
And heard his Maker's voice,'

I suppose he was not more than six or seven years old. And Moses, and David, and Jeremiah, and John the Baptist, and Timothy, began to seek God even earlier than that. God says to each of you, my young friends, '*Now* is the accepted time, now is the day of salvation.' If you only ask God to help you by His grace and Holy Spirit, you may begin at once to seek, and to serve the blessed Saviour. When He speaks in the text of our seeking Him 'early,' He does not mean at any particular age. This leaves the way open for any or all of us to begin to seek God at once, however young we may be. No one need wait another day or hour. And the promise is, 'Those who seek Me early shall find Me.' And when we find Jesus, as our friend and Saviour, who can tell what it is we find in Him? We have heard of men finding gold mines, or diamond mines; and those who do so are considered very fortunate. But suppose that all the gold, and silver, and diamond mines in the world were united in one; and suppose that that one mine had been discovered by some favoured individual, and that all its treasures belonged to him; how much he would be envied! And yet, to find God would be infinitely better for us, than to find that mine. The treasures of that mine would soon perish, or pass away; but the good things we find in God will last for ever, and make us always happy.

Our sermon to-day will be about the *promise of finding God.* And there are *three* good things we are sure to have, when we find Him.

The first of these is—PARDON.

What a blessing pardon is, we never can understand, till we feel the burden of our sins. We never can tell what a blessing food is, till we are hungry. We never can tell how much the cool, clear water from the fountain is worth, till we are parched with thirst. We never know how valuable medicine is, till we are suffering from the pains of sickness. And so it is with pardon. It is only when we find out what a terrible evil sin is; when we know that God is angry with us, on account of it; and that we never can be happy till we get our sins forgiven: only *then* can we see, and feel, that pardon is the greatest of all blessings. Suppose that a man had a poisonous serpent coiled around his body. It is biting, and stinging him all the time. Could he have any comfort day or night? Not at all. He might be worth millions of money, and be living in one of the finest houses in the country; but he could not find any enjoyment either from his money or his home. The one thing which that man would need, above everything else, would be, to get rid of that biting, stinging serpent. Here is a good story to illustrate this point of our subject. We may call it—

THE POWER OF THE BLOOD.

A traveller in India fell asleep one night, upon the damp, warm ground. Early in the morning, he was awakened by feeling pricking, stinging pains all over the surface of his body.

On getting up to see what was the matter, he found that a swarm of big grey leeches had fastened on his flesh, and were busy sucking up his blood. They gave him a great deal of pain, and he felt that he never could enjoy anything till he got rid of him. The first thing that he thought of doing was to tear them of with his hand.

But a native servant, acquainted with the ways of the country, when he saw what he was about to do, came up to him, and said: 'Please, master, don't do that. If you tear them off in that way, parts of their bodies will remain in your flesh, and breed corruption and decay, that will cause you great suffering. Wait a little while, and I will get them all off for you, without any trouble.'

Then he went and got a particular kind of herb. He steeped it in warm water, and then brought it to his master. Putting his hand into this basin of water, he gently bathed the different parts of the body, to which the leeches were clinging; and very soon they all dropped quietly off, and the traveller was relieved.

Now when that poor man awoke from sleep, and found those leeches clinging to him, giving him so much pain, and threatening him with such serious consequences, we may well regard him as representing our condition, when we wake up to see what sinners we are, and what danger we are in from our sins. The great thing which that man needed was to be rid of his leeches. He could have had no comfort in anything till that end was secured. And the great thing that we need, as sinners, is to have our sins pardoned, and so to get rid of all the sad consequences which must follow if they are not put away.

But how are we to do this? It was the application of that prepared water which relieved the man of his leeches; and so, it is the application of the precious blood of Christ to our souls that will secure to us the pardon of our sins, and save us from all the sad consequences that must follow if they are not pardoned.

I have one other story here, to show that when men feel the burden of their sins they know that pardon is the greatest blessing they can receive; and that until they obtain it they never can be happy. And then, there is nothing in the world that they would not be willing to do in order to secure this pardon.

Some time ago, an English missionary in India was

preaching to a company of Hindoos, in a grove, by the roadside. The text from which he was speaking was 1 John i. 7: 'And the blood of Jesus Christ His Son cleanseth us from all sin.' Among his hearers was a Hindoo, in just the state of feeling of which we have been speaking. He was burdened under a sense of his sins, and desired, above all things, to get rid of this burden. He was willing to go anywhere, and do anything, if he could only get his sins pardoned. He had consulted several priests, of the Hindoo religion, in which he had been brought up. One of them advised him to go and wash himself seven times in the sacred river Ganges. He went and washed; but found no relief. At the advice of other priests he visited different temples, one after another, and made costly offerings there, but it was all in vain. His burden still pressed upon him. He could get no pardon for his sins. He was now on his way to a temple several hundred miles distant. He had been told that he must go there on foot, with pebble stones in his shoes. The priest told him that this would please the god of that temple, and perhaps he would give him the pardon he so much desired. His feet were already so very sore, that every step he took caused him very great suffering.

This poor man was wonderfully interested in listening to the words of the missionary. After the service was over he waited to see him, and to hear more about the way of salvation that is in Jesus. The missionary's words to him were like cold water to a thirsty soul. He drank them in with unspeakable delight. He embraced the Saviour, as the missionary made Him known to him. Then, taking off his shoes, he threw away the pebbles that were in them, saying as he did so: 'No more journeys to idol temples. Jesus is the true God. Pardon through His blood! This meets my wants. This is what I have long sought, but sought in vain. I have found it now, and it makes me perfectly happy!'

This man sought Jesus as soon as he knew about Him. He sought him as early as he could, and found Him. And in finding Him, he found the greatest of all blessings—the pardon of his sins.

The first good thing promised to those who find Jesus is—*pardon.*

The second good thing promised to those who find Jesus is—PEACE.

Jesus is called—'the Prince of Peace.' When the angels sang their song of gladness over His birth, they spoke of Him as having come to bring 'peace on earth.' His gospel is called 'the gospel of peace.' The Apostle Paul tells us that when we become Christians, by exercising faith in Jesus, we 'have peace with God.' With the *wicked*—and this means all of us till we become Christians—'God is angry every day.' How dreadful it is to think of a great Being like God, from whom we can never get away, who is always present everywhere, and who is able to make all things work together to do us harm,—how dreadful it is to think of such a Being as angry with us! And yet, until we seek and find Jesus, *this* is just the way that God feels towards us. But to know that God is at peace with us; that He thinks and feels kindly towards us; that He is trying in every way to bless us; and, as St. Paul says, is making all 'things work together for our good:' can there possibly be any greater comfort than this? And yet, when we seek Jesus early, as our text says—*this* is what we find in Him. He makes peace with us, and becomes our friend for time and for eternity. This is enough to encourage every one to seek Him.

Let us look at some illustrations of the wonderful

effect of that peace which Jesus gives to those who find him. The first we may call—

THE BRIGHT SIDE.

A Christian lady came home from a walk one day, and said to her sister: 'Jeannie, dear, I have just been taught one of the best lessons I have ever learned. It has been like a sermon to me.'

'Do tell me all about it,' said her sister.

'Well, just before I turned the corner, on my way home, I met our afflicted friend Mrs. Jackson. We stopped and chatted awhile; and as we parted, with a beautiful smile lighting her patient face, she said: "I am so glad I met you, Mary, dear, for it will be something cheering to tell Bessie about, when I get home. Bessie says, 'There's always something pleasant.' Good-bye." As soon as she was gone I said to myself, "How can poor Mrs. Jackson be so patient, and cheerful?" You know what she has passed through. Once she had everything the world could give, to make her comfortable and happy. Now, she has lost all the world can take away from her. Her husband—her health—her property—her friends have all been taken from her. The only family tie left to her is poor Bessie. But she suffers greatly from a spine disease, and is totally blind! And yet, Mrs. Jackson never complains, whatever happens; while poor Bessie says, "There's always something pleasant." You know they are both Christians. They have sought and found Jesus. And the lesson I have just learned, is about the kind of blessing they have received from Him. It is something which can help them to bear their heavy trials so patiently, and which can lead Bessie, notwithstanding the suffering from her spine, and her blindness, to say, "There's always something pleasant." I hope I shall always remember the lesson I have learned to-day; and try never to worry, or complain, whatever may happen.'

That is a good lesson for us all to learn. And the blessing we shall find in Jesus, when we get the *pardon* and the *peace* He gives, will help us to feel and act just as Mrs. Jackson and her daughter Bessie did.

They were only doing what the prophet Habakkuk did, when he said: 'Although the fig-tree shall not blossom, neither shall fruit be in the vines; the labour of the olive shall fail, and the fields shall yield no meat; the flock shall be cut off from the fold, and there shall be no herd in the stalls: *Yet* I will rejoice in the Lord, and joy in the God of my salvation.' That good prophet had sought and found God, and the blessing he received from Him was enough to make him happy, when he had lost everything else.

Our next illustration may be called—

A SCENE IN INDIA.

'One evening about sunset,' says an English missionary in India, 'I was walking with one of the native members of my church. In the course of our walk we passed near a large village. As we went by, my companion pointed to a small hut, in the outskirts of the village, and said: "In yonder hut is the only Christian to be found in this village. Ten years ago he sought and found the Saviour. But ever since then he has had great trials to bear. His father and mother turned him out of their home. His friends forsook him; his neighbours persecuted him; and during all those years, he has found it hard work to support himself, and get a living. But he has stood his ground manfully, and maintained a consistent Christian character, all that time. And the heathen around him have learned to have confidence in him; and his business is reviving; for the people say he sells the best things, and always means just what he says."

'I made up my mind,' said the missionary, 'to go and see this Hindoo Christian as soon as possible. So a day or two after our conversation, I made him a visit. From what had been told me, about the way in which he had been forsaken and persecuted, I thought of course that he must be feeling very lonely and sad. In my conversation with him, I spoke of his loneliness and sadness, and tried to say such things as would be likely to comfort one who was having such feelings. But to my surprise, with his eyes full of tears, he looked me earnestly in the face, and said,—

'"Oh, sir, please don't talk to me in that way. How can I feel lonely, when Jesus is always with me, as He was with the three Hebrews in the fiery furnace, and with Daniel in the lions' den? And how can I feel sad, when I know, as the Apostle Paul says, that He is making all things work together for my good."

'I looked at the man with wonder,' said the missionary. 'And then I said to myself, What a blessing this poor man has found in Jesus! It is a blessing that can take the place of all other things.'

This man's experience is just such as some one has described in these sweet lines—

'Lonely, dear Lord! how can I be
With Thy sweet presence here?
Thy strength in weakness to make strong;
Thy hand to wipe each tear?

'Lonely, dear Lord! I only am
When wandering from Thy side;
But heaviest crosses light become
If I in Thee abide.

'AN OFFICER SAW THE POOR MAN.'

'O blessèd Saviour! faithful Friend,
When earthly friends forsake,
Thy presence lights life's darkest hour,
And earth a heaven doth make.'

There is one other illustration, which we may call—

THE DYING SOLDIER.

'Put me down,' said a wounded Prussian soldier, at the battle of Sedan, to his companions, who were carrying him away; 'put me down, I'm dying. Don't trouble yourselves to carry me any further.'

They put him down and returned to the fight. A few minutes after an officer saw the poor man weltering in his blood, and said to him, 'Can I do anything for you, my friend?'

'No, thank you, sir. I am dying.'

'Shall I get you a drink of water?' said the kind-hearted officer.

'No, thank you, sir.'

'Is there nothing I can do for you?'

'There is one thing for which I would be much obliged to you. Please open my knapsack. You will find a New Testament there. Open it at the fourteenth chapter of St. John. Near the end of the chapter you will find a verse about "Peace." Please read it.'

The officer did so, and read the words: 'Peace I leave with you; My peace I give unto you. Let not your heart be troubled, neither let it be afraid.'

'Thank you, sir,' said the dying man. 'I have that peace; I am going to that Saviour. I want no more. These were his last words. That man had sought and found Jesus. And the peace which He gave him in his dying hour met his wants, and made him happy, as nothing else in the world could have done.

The second good thing promised to those who find Jesus is *peace.*

The third good thing promised to them is—PROSPERITY.

This does not mean that when we begin to serve God He will always make us successful in our business, and cause us to become rich in worldly things. But it means that, in addition to the pardon and peace which He promises, He will give us all the help and grace we need to make us good and happy. And this is the best kind of prosperity. It is a thousand times better to have the grace of God working effectually in our souls, than to have all the gold, and silver, and worldly wealth that it is possible to gain. And from the time when we seek and find Jesus, *this* is just what we may expect. God's promise to each of us is: 'From *this day* will I bless you' (Hag. ii. 19). This means from the day when we begin to love and serve Him. And it is true, as Solomon says, 'that the blessing of the Lord, it maketh rich, and He addeth no sorrow.' If God sees that it will be best for any of us to be rich in this world's goods, then His blessing will be sure to make us so. But if He sees that if we are rich in worldly things, our souls will not prosper, then God will leave us poor in the things of this world, but, as St. Paul says, 'rich in faith, and heirs of His glorious kingdom.' But when we seek, and find God, we may be very sure that His blessing will follow us, and secure to us just the kind of prosperity which He sees will be the best for us. Sometimes God makes His people prosperous in worldly things, as well as in those that are spiritual. At other times He keeps them back from worldly prosperity, but makes their souls to prosper. We have illustrations in the Bible of both these kinds of prosperity. We have a good illustration of the experience of worldly prosperity in the case of Joseph. He sought God early, and found Him. And wonderful the prosperity was which followed Joseph! He had indeed a very trying path to walk in, before he reached the prosperity that awaited him. He was cruelly torn away from the arms of his loving father, by his unfeeling brethren. He was sold as a slave into Egypt. Who can tell what trials of feeling Joseph must have had, in passing through all this part of his history? He was successful there for a little while; and then, on a false accusation, he was cast into prison. He was kept there for several years. Yet even there he was prosperous; for the Lord was with him, and he had the charge of everything there. But one day, from that gloomy prison he rose, at a single bound, to the highest position in Egypt, next to that of King Pharaoh. He rode in the second chariot in the kingdom; and they cried before him, 'Bow the knee.' Until the day of his death he was the greatest, the most honoured and prosperous man in all the land of Egypt. Surely Joseph found prosperity in serving God.

And then in Daniel we have another illustration of the same kind of prosperity. When a youth he was carried captive to Babylon. He was poor, and unknown, and no one ever expected that he would be successful there. But, like Joseph, he had sought God early, and found Him. And God blessed him with the most surprising prosperity. He rose from one position of honour and dignity to another, till, like Joseph in Egypt, he stood next to the king, in what was then the mightiest kingdom in the world. And he continued in that high office, not through one reign only, but through the reigns of several successive kings. What a prosperous man Daniel was both in temporal and spiritual things!

And then we have a Bible illustration of one of God's servants who had no prosperity in worldly things, but who was wonderfully prosperous in spiritual things. I refer to the Apostle Paul. Before his conversion he had the prospect of great honours and riches. But when he became a Christian those bright prospects faded away. He endured the loss of all earthly things. He never had any worldly prosperity. But he was wonderfully prosperous in all spiritual things. He was a very giant of a Christian. Next to our blessed Lord Himself, no one ever lived who did so much good as St. Paul did. And how happy he was in doing his work, we see in one little incident mentioned of him. In the city of Philippi, on a certain occasion, he was put in prison for preaching the gospel. His feet were made fast in the stocks, and his back was torn and bleeding from the stripes which had been laid upon him; yet still he spent the night in singing, out of the gladness of his heart, to the glory and praise of God. A prosperous man St. Paul was in all that pertained to his soul.

And when we seek and find Jesus, we shall have prosperity in one, or other, or both of the ways that we have spoken of. If God wants us to have worldly prosperity, He expects us to act in such a way as will help to secure it. Joseph did this; and so did Daniel. And we must do the same, if we hope to prosper in our worldly affairs.

I have just one short incident to illustrate this point of our subject. We may call it—

HOW A BOY PROSPERED.

Robbie Davis was a lad about ten years old. But, young as he was, he had sought and found the Saviour. He was expecting to prosper, and was trying to do all he could to secure the prosperity that he desired. His mother was a poor widow, unable to support him, and he had made up his mind, with his mother's consent, to try and get a situation on board a ship and go to sea. So going down to one of the wharves in Boston, where he lived, he went up to a well known merchant, and said: 'Sir, have you any situation on board your ship? I want to earn something.'

'What can you do?' asked the merchant.

'I can try to do whatever I am told to do,' was the boy's answer.

'What *have* you done?'

'I have sawed and split all mother's wood, for nigh on to two years.'

'And what have you *not* done?' asked the gentleman, who had a queer way of putting things.

'Well, sir,' said the boy, after a moment's pause, 'I haven't whispered once in school for a whole year.'

'That's enough,' said the merchant. 'You may ship aboard this vessel; and I hope to see you the captain of her some day. A boy who can master a wood-pile, and bridle his tongue, is made of good stuff, and is bound to prosper.'

Now we have spoken of three blessings which God promises to give to those who seek Him early, and find Him. The first is *pardon*; the second is *peace*; and the third is *prosperity*.

But, when compared to all the blessings that are found in Jesus, these are only like three drops of water taken out of the ocean. There is no end to the blessings He has to give to His people. I will close this sermon with some very precious lines on this subject. I do not know by whom they are written. But I never get tired of repeating them. They are called—

WHAT CHRIST IS TO THOSE WHO KNOW HIM.

'What the breast is at the birth,
What the soil is to the earth,
What the gem is to the mine,

What the grape is to the vine,
What the bloom is to the tree,
That—is Jesus Christ to me.

'What the string is to the lute,
What the breath is to the flute,
What the spring is to the watch,
What the nerve is to the touch,
What the breeze is to the sea,
That—is Jesus Christ to me.

'What the estate is to the heir,
What the autumn to the year,
What the seed is to the farm,
What the sunbeam to the corn,
What the flower is to the bee,
That—is Jesus Christ to me.

'What the light is to the eye,
What the sun is to the sky,
What the sea is to the river,
What the hand is to the giver,
What a friend is to the plea,
That—is Jesus Christ to me.

'What culture is unto the waste,
What honey is unto the taste,
What fragrance is unto the smell
Or springs of water to a well,
What beauty is in all I see,
All this, and more, is Christ to me.

VI.

THE PROMISED BLESSING.

'From this day will I bless you.'—HAG. ii. 19.

THE prophet Haggai lived about five hundred years before the birth of our Saviour. Many years before he wrote the words of our text, the king of Babylon had sent a great army against Jerusalem, and destroyed it. The beautiful temple which Solomon built, for the worship of God, had been left in ruins; and the people of Israel had been carried captives to Babylon. After that captivity had lasted for seventy years, the people had been allowed to return to their own country. Large numbers of them had gone back. The walls of Jerusalem, and many of its dwelling-houses, had been rebuilt. But the temple of God was still in ruins. The prophet Haggai had been sent by God to encourage the people of Israel to rebuild that temple. At first they were unwilling to begin this work. But after the prophet had talked to them about it, they made up their minds to obey the command of God, and to begin to build the temple. Then God sent to them, by the prophet, the precious promise which we have taken for our present text. He said to them—'From this day will I bless you.' Just as soon as they determined to keep God's commandment, and do what He told them to do, God said He would bless them. And He says the same to each of us.

Our souls are like temples. The Apostle Paul, in writing to the Corinthian Christians, said, 'Ye are the temple of the living God' (2 Cor. vi. 16). But sin has left the temple of our souls in ruins. God wishes to have these temples repaired, for His glory and for our good. And when any of us begin to love and serve God, then, like the Jews in the time of the prophet Haggai, we are beginning to rebuild God's temple that was in ruins. This is what God wants us to do. And He gives us the same promise that He gave to the Jews. When we begin in earnest, to love and serve Him, and so to rebuild the ruined temple of our souls, He says to each of us, 'From this day will I bless you.'

Our sermon to-day is about *the blessing promised to those who serve God.* And if you ask what God's blessing will do for us? I wish to speak of *three* things that it does for all who receive it.

In the first place, 'the blessing of the Lord' will make us —RICH.

In the tenth chapter of the book of Proverbs, and the twenty-second verse, Solomon says, 'The blessing of the Lord maketh rich.' But this does not mean, that when we begin to serve God we are sure to have plenty of gold, and silver, and worldly possessions. The meaning is that God's blessing will make us rich, by giving us His love, and grace, and favour, so that we shall be truly happy. We often see men, who are very rich in the things of this world, but yet are wretched and miserable.

We have a good illustration of this part of our subject in our Saviour's parable of the rich man and Lazarus.

The rich man, we are told, was clothed in purple and fine linen, and fared sumptuously every day. No doubt he had plenty of servants to wait upon him; and he rode in his carriage, whenever he wanted to go anywhere.

But Lazarus was a poor beggar. He was laid every

day at the rich man's gate, asking to be fed with the crumbs which fell from the rich man's table; and his body was full of sores. Now, if *this* was all we knew of these two men, and any one should ask us which of them we would rather be? it would be natural to say, 'Why, the rich man of course.' But if we should wait a little while, till Jesus tells us some more about them, we should change our minds. The parable goes on to say, that by and by the beggar died, and was carried by the angels into Abraham's bosom. That was the way in which the Jews used to speak of heaven. Abraham was the father of their nation. They thought him the best and the greatest man that ever lived. And to get near to him, and especially to lean on his bosom, as Lazarus did, they thought was the best and happiest place in heaven. But it was *just there* that the angels carried Lazarus when he died.

And not long after that, we are told, 'the rich man also died; and was buried.' He had, no doubt, a costly funeral. But did the angels carry him to Abraham's bosom? Ah! no. For the next thing we hear about him is—that he went to the bad place. There he was in great torment. And when he lifted up his eyes, he saw Abraham in heaven, and Lazarus—the poor beggar, that used to sit at his gate every day, when they were on earth—'in Abraham's bosom.' And then he offered up a prayer to him, and said, 'I pray thee, father Abraham, that thou wouldest send Lazarus, that he may dip the tip of his finger in water, and cool my tongue: for I am tormented in this flame.' But Abraham said, 'Son, remember, that thou in thy lifetime receivedst thy good things, and Lazarus evil things; but now he is comforted, and thou art tormented.' And then he told him, that there was a great gulf fixed, between the place where Lazarus was and where he was, so that it was impossible to pass from one of them to the other.

Now, which of these two men was the best off? Lazarus, of course. What good did the rich man's money do him in that place of torment? None at all. He could not buy one drop of water to cool his tongue, in the flame from which he was suffering. But how different it was with Lazarus! He had 'the blessing of the Lord;' and it made him rich indeed. He had everything he could desire to make him happy. Lazarus was the rich man then. And he is rich in heaven to-day; yes, and he will be so for ever.

I have another illustration of this part of our subject. It is something like our Saviour's parable of the rich man and Lazarus. We may call it—

RICH IN FAITH.

One day a wealthy English gentleman was riding on horseback, over his large estate. Suddenly he drew up the bridle to stop his horse. Then he listened, as he thought he heard some one speaking. On looking over the hedge, he saw a poor man, who had long been employed in breaking stones on his roads, and who was generally called 'John the stone-breaker.' Looking at him a moment, the rich man said, 'John, you fool, what are you talking to yourself about?'

'Please, sir,' said John, 'I wasn't speaking to myself. I was just asking God's blessing on my dinner.'

'Ha! ha!' laughed the rich man; 'and pray what have you got for your dinner, John?'

'Well, sir,' replied John, 'I've only got a crust of bread, and a mug of pure water from the brook; but, sir, it's a dainty meal with God's blessing on it.'

'Well, well,' said his master, 'you can do as you please; but it would be a long time before I would ask God's blessing on such a dinner as that. I wish you much good from the blessing, John.' And then he rode off.

Still John enjoyed his dinner. And with the blessing of God in his heart, making him feel happy now, in spite of his poverty; and happier still in the hope of heaven, he felt that he was much better off than his rich master, who knew nothing of Jesus and His love.

One afternoon, not long after this, John's rich master was walking in his garden, when he thought he heard some one say, '*The richest man in the county will die to-night.*' This startled him very much. For, supposing that *he* was the richest man in the county, he said to himself, 'Is it possible that *I* must die to-night?' This alarmed him greatly.

He hurried home at once. Then he sent for his lawyer, and his physician. When they arrived he was in bed, in a state of great excitement. He called the lawyer to his bedside first, to settle all his business matters. When this was done the lawyer went off.

Then he called to his physician, and asked him, very earnestly, to do all he could to save his life. The doctor was greatly surprised. He felt his pulse. He examined his tongue, and asked him a number of questions. These were all answered satisfactorily. Then he said, 'Why, my friend, there is nothing the matter with you. You are perfectly well.'

But in great alarm he declared, 'You must be mistaken, Doctor. I shall die before the morning.'

The trouble with him was, that he was terribly frightened at the thought of dying. He felt that he was a sinner; and that with his sins all unpardoned, he was not prepared to meet his God.

The doctor gave him some medicine to make him sleep, and promised to stay with him through the night. But he never slept a wink. He was tossing restlessly on his bed, all the night.

As soon as the morning dawned, the doctor advised him to get up, and go out, and take a walk before breakfast. He did go out, pale and trembling, and fearing that at every step he might drop down dead. He had not gone far, however, before he was met by one of the poor men who worked on his farm. Taking off his cap, and making a polite bow, he said,—

'Please, sir, may I speak to you?'

'Of course you may. What have you to say?'

'Well, sir,' said the man, 'I thought I would like to tell you that poor John, the stone-breaker, died last night.'

'What's that?' exclaimed the rich man, in the greatest possible surprise. 'John, the stone-breaker, dead! Ah! I see it now—I see it now. What a fool I was, to think that my broad acres, my splendid house, and my gold and silver, made me the richest man in the county. But it was not so. I was mistaken. Poor John, the stone-breaker, was the man. It was "the blessing of the Lord" which he had, that made him the richest man in the county!'

God's promise to us, when we begin to serve Him, is —'From this day will I bless you.' And the first thing that this blessing does for us is to make us rich.

The second thing that this blessing does for us is, to make us—GOOD.

The best blessing we can ever have, is that which will make us really good. Nothing that the world can give will be of much use to us, unless we can get our hearts changed, and made good.

We have a good illustration of this in the case of Naaman, the Syrian, of whom we read in 2 Kings 5th chapter. There we are told that—"Naaman, captain of the host of the king of Syria, was a great man with his master, and honourable, because by him the Lord had given deliverance to Syria; he was also a mighty man in valour,—but he was a leper.' He had great riches; great honour; great success as a soldier; he had all that the world could give him in the way of blessing,—but what good could it all do for him, while he was suffering from that terrible disease—the leprosy? Among the Jews, lepers were not allowed to keep company with other people. They were obliged to live by themselves, for fear they might give the disease to other people by touching them. Sometimes the leprosy would break out in terrible sores, in different parts of the body; and it would make the fingers and toes decay, and fall off, till the limbs of the poor sufferers would, as it were, be eaten away. How unhappy this dreadful disease must have made poor Naaman feel, in spite of all his greatness! How gladly he would have given up all his riches, and all his honours, if he could only have gotten rid of his leprosy!

And just what that leprosy was to Naaman, sin is to us. It is the disease of our souls. It pollutes them, as the leprosy polluted the bodies of those who had it. It makes us unfit for heaven, and for the company of the holy angels. All the riches, and honours, and greatness in the world can never make us happy, unless we can get rid of our sins. But when we get that blessing of the Lord, spoken of in our text, *this* is just what it will do for us. It changes our hearts, and makes us good. St. Paul says, 'If any man be in Christ, he is a *new creature.*' And when this change takes place, we are made *like Jesus.* This is to be made good indeed. It is the best kind of goodness. This blessing will not only *make* us good, but it will help us to grow better and better the longer we live; and at last, it will make us—'perfect, even as our Father in heaven is perfect.'

How great that blessing is, which can secure a change like this, to poor sinful creatures such as we are! And how well God may say to us, when we come to Jesus, 'From this day will I bless you.'

Here are some illustrations of persons who had received this blessing, and were made good by it. The first is about—

A GOOD LITTLE BOY.

He was about ten years old. His name was Willie Jones. He had given his heart to the Saviour, and was trying to be a Christian. God had given him the blessing that makes His people good.

'One cold slippery day in winter,' says a Christian lady, 'I was sitting at my window, watching the people as they passed along the street. The walking was dangerous, and I saw several people fall. There was a very slippery place not far from my window, and a lot of boys standing near it, laughing and talking and making snowballs. Presently a little girl came along, carrying a basket on her arm, full of buttons, tapes, papers of pins, shoe-strings and the like. Just as she reached the dangerous place spoken of above, she slipped, and fell on the pavement. Her basket was upset, and all the things in it rolled out on the ice and snow. I thought some of the boys, who were near, would go up and help the poor child. But they didn't. They only laughed at her, and went on with their play. But I had seen my neighbour, little Willie Jones, a short time before, looking out of the window of their house, right across the street. I knew Willie was a good boy, and I expected to see him come out and help this poor child. And so he did. For as I looked up I saw him, without overcoat or mittens, hurrying across the street. He first helped the little girl to her feet; then he carefully gathered up all the things that had rolled out of her basket, and put them safely back there. And not satisfied with that, but finding that she was stiff, and suffering from the cold, he asked her to come over to his mother's house, to warm herself, and have something to eat, before going on her way. The poor child was glad enough to go; and in the course of half an hour, or so, I saw her come out of Mrs. Jones's house, looking cheerful and happy.'

Now surely 'the blessing of the Lord' had made Willie Jones a good boy. He was trying faithfully to follow the example of that blessed Saviour who, when He was on earth, 'went about doing good.'

Our next illustration may be called—

THE GOOD CHINAMAN.

A missionary at Ningpo, one day, saw a respectable-looking Chinaman in his mission-room, whom he had never seen there before. After the service was over, he went up and shook hands with him.

In the course of his conversation, the missionary said to him, 'My friend, have you ever heard the gospel preached before?'

'No, sir,' he replied; 'but I have *seen* it preached.' And then he went on to explain his meaning, in this way: 'I know a man who used to be the terror of his neighbourhood. If you spoke a cross word to him, he would shout at you, and keep on cursing you without ceasing, for ever so long. He was a bad opium-smoker, and was as dangerous as a wild beast. But when the religion of Jesus took hold of him, he became entirely changed. He has left off smoking opium. He is honest and true. You can depend on everything he says. He is kind and gentle; and from being the worst man in the neighbourhood, he is now the best. You talk about *hearing* the gospel preached; but it is like *seeing* the gospel preached to watch the life of that man. And I believe in the religion which can make so good a man out of one who used to be so bad.'

I have one other illustration for this part of our sermon. We may call it—

AN INDIAN'S IDEA OF GOODNESS.

There was a celebrated Indian chief, whose name was Tedyscung. He was king of the Delaware tribe of Indians.

One evening he was sitting at the fireside of a friend. They did not seem disposed to talk much, but both were busy thinking. At length his friend spoke out and said: 'Let me tell you what I have been thinking about. The Lord Jesus Christ, the author of the Christian religion, left His followers a rule, which they call—*The Golden Rule.* I think it is the best rule I ever heard of.'

'Stop,' said Tedyscung, 'don't go on praising it, before I know what it is. Let me hear it, and think for myself. Don't tell me how good it is, but tell me *what* it is.'

'It is this,' said his friend, 'that one man should do to another, just what he would have the other do to him.'

'That's impossible. It cannot be done,' said Tedyscung. Then they were both silent again. Presently Tedyscung lighted his pipe, and walked up and down the room, thinking earnestly of that golden rule, about which they had been talking. After awhile he came up to his friend, and sitting down by his side, he took his pipe out of his mouth, and said, as a smile played over his face—'Brother, I have been thinking of what you said about that golden rule. If the Great Spirit, that made man, should give him a *new heart*, *then* he could do as you say, but he never can do it without that.'

That Indian chief was right. But the blessing of the Lord, promised in our text, will do this very thing for us. It will change our hearts and make us good. And then it will be easy for us to keep the golden rule, or any other rule that God gives us.

The second thing that this blessing does for us is to make us *good*.

The third thing that this blessing does for us is, to make us—GREAT.

There are two kinds of greatness: one is greatness in the sight of men; the other is greatness in the sight of God. The first of these is not worth much. Men sometimes call persons great for doing things that are very wrong. There, for example, were Julius Cæsar, and Alexander the Great, and Napoleon Bonaparte. They are counted among the great ones of the earth. And yet, the principal thing for which they were counted great was—the number of people they killed. They were soldiers. They won famous victories. But *how* did they win those victories? It was by wading through rivers of blood. I suppose that each of those great men caused the death of more than a million of people. Who would care to have greatness like theirs, that was all stained with blood? Those men did not pretend to be *good*; but they did think themselves *great*. All the world calls them great; but nobody pretends to call them good. In the sight of men many persons are called great who are never considered good. Christopher Columbus was called a great man because he discovered America. He might have been a very good man. I do not say he was not. But a person may have that sort of greatness, without being good at all. Many men have been called great for the inventions they have made, or for certain things they have done, without any thought of what their own character was. But God's blessing always makes His people good, at the same time that it makes them great. This goodness and greatness always go together.

God makes His people great by *making them like Himself.* And He is the highest model of greatness.

And then another way in which God makes His people great is by bringing them *very near to Himself.* In countries like England, where they have a king or queen at the head of the government, those persons whose office or duty brings them nearest to the king, or queen, are considered the most honoured, or the greatest. When the angel was sent to foretell the birth of John the Baptist, to his father Zacharias, he said to him, in giving an account of himself, 'I am Gabriel, that stand in the presence of God.' This was the best proof of his greatness. And if we have the blessing of God, spoken of in our text, we shall share the same greatness. Jesus said of all His people, 'They shall be equal to the angels.' There is no greatness that men can give which can for a moment be compared with this.

And then there is one other thing that Jesus will do for His people, which shows how wonderful their greatness will be! *He will share His throne and His glory with them.*

This is what no earthly king ever did for one of his people. But Jesus will do it for all who love and serve Him. He says Himself, 'To him that overcometh'—this means to every faithful servant of His—'will I give to sit down with Me on My throne, even as I also overcame, and am set down with My Father on His throne.' This is the highest point of greatness that any creature of God can ever reach. And when we think of this we see how truly it may be said of the blessing of the Lord, that it makes His people great.

Aunt Judy.—*Page* 103.

Let us look now at some illustrations of this greatness. The first we may call—

THE CHRISTIAN'S GLORY.

In a certain village in New England there lived a good old Christian lady, whom everybody that knew her respected and loved. She was known, among her friends, as Aunt Judy. No matter what happened, she always was bright and cheerful; and had a pleasant word to say to every one. A friend of hers called to see her one day. She was a very changeable person. One day she would be cheerful; and the next day she would be dull and gloomy. At one time she would be kind and pleasant; at another she would be cross and disagreeable. As they were talking together this neighbour said, 'Aunt Judy, don't you sometimes change?'

'Yes, I do,' was her reply.

'Well, I thought it must be so,' said her friend. 'I suppose everybody must change occasionally; sometimes they are up, and then again they are down. At one time they feel cheerful and happy; and at another they feel sad and sorrowful.'

'Ah! but that is not the way I change, my friend,' said Aunt Judy. 'I only know of but one change, thank God! and that is the change from glory to glory.'

And if we are the true servants of God, this will be the only change we shall ever know, either in this world or in the world to come. What an interesting view this gives us of heaven! This was what Solomon meant when he said, 'The path of the just is as the shining light, that shineth more and more unto the perfect day.' Only think of the soul of the Christian, for thousands and thousands of years, going on 'from glory to glory,'—and who can imagine what the greatness of that state will be?

Our next illustration may be called—

WHAT A KING THOUGHT OF THIS GREATNESS.

On one occasion the king of Prussia was visiting a certain village in that country. A committee of the school children had been appointed to meet the king, and bid him welcome to their village. Their teacher, who was with them, made a nice little speech to the king. Then the king thanked the children for their kind welcome, and spoke some pleasant words to them. He was standing by the table on which were the refreshments provided for the occasion.

Picking up an orange from a plate, he held it towards the children, and then asked,—

'To what kingdom does this belong, my dear children?'

'To the vegetable kingdom, please your majesty,' said a bright little girl.

Then the king took a gold coin from his pocket, and holding it up, asked,—

'And to what kingdom does this belong?'

'To the mineral kingdom,' said the little girl.

And then, laying his hand on his breast, he asked,—

'And to what kingdom do I belong?'

The little girl blushed, and was at a loss for an answer. She didn't like to say—to the *animal* kingdom; for she was afraid the king would be offended if she called him an animal. Then the thought came into her mind that 'God made man in His own image,' and so, looking up with a sweet smile, she said, 'You belong to God's kingdom, please your majesty.'

This touched the heart of the king. His eyes filled with tears; and for a moment or two he could not speak. And then, going up to the little girl, he laid his hand gently on her head, and said, with much feeling, 'God grant, my dear child, that you and I may both be counted worthy, through the merits of Christ, to share the greatness of that kingdom!'

I have only one other illustration. We may call it—

WHAT A MINISTER THOUGHT OF THIS GREATNESS.

Two hundred years ago there was a celebrated minister, at Paris, in France. He was the most eloquent and popular preacher ever known in that country. On the death of Louis XIV., king of France, Massillon, this famous preacher, was called upon to preach the dead king's funeral sermon. The service was held in the old Cathedral of Notre-Dame. The large building was crowded with people. The new king, Louis XV., and all the nobility of France were present. The great congregation was seated, and waiting for the minister to appear. The silence of death was there. Massillon entered, and walked to the sacred desk, holding in his left hand a little golden urn, in which was a lock of hair belonging to the dead king. He stood by the desk in silence, holding up the little urn. Moment after moment passed away, and he stood there pale and silent as a statue. The feeling became intense. Some thought he was afraid to speak before that vast assembly; others sighed and groaned aloud. At last the hand of the preacher was seen slowly raising the golden urn, and with his eyes fixed on the new king, his clear, solemn voice was distinctly heard in every part of that great Cathedral, uttering these startling words: '*God alone is great.*' The greatness of the dead king had passed away like a dream. Massillon wished to set in contrast to *that*, the greatness that will never pass away. And this was why he uttered those solemn words—'God alone is great.' But if we secure the blessing spoken of in our text, then this greatness will be ours.

Our sermon to-day is about the blessing promised to those who serve God. And we have spoken of *three* things this blessing will do for us. It will make us *rich;* it will make us *good;* and it will make us *great.* Let us all seek this blessing, and then it will be well with us, for time and for eternity.

VII.

HOW CHRISTIANS ARE A BLESSING.

'*And thou shalt be a blessing.*'—Gen. xii. 2.

This was God's promise to Abraham when He first called him to be His servant, and made a covenant with him. But the promise here given was not intended for Abraham alone. It is meant to apply to all, who, like Abraham, become the true servants of God. If you and I are really loving and serving God, then, to each of us God says, '*Thou* shalt be a blessing.' Just look at some of the ways in which God speaks of His people in the Bible, and that will show us what real blessings they are. What a blessing light is! But Jesus calls His people—'the light of the world' (Matt. v. 14). What a blessing salt is! But Jesus calls His people—'the salt of the earth' (Matt. v. 13). Lambs, and doves, and wheat, and palm trees, and cedar trees have been blessings to men, but these are things to which God compares His people. Gold and jewels, when rightly used, are blessings, and God compares His people to these things. What blessings good kings and good priests and ministers have been to the world! But God tells us that all His people will be kings and priests unto Him (Rev. i. 6).

Our sermon to-day is about—*how Christians are a blessing.*

We might speak of a great many ways in which they are so. But we have only time to speak of three ways in which every true Christian will prove a blessing, wherever he may be.

The first way in which God makes His people a blessing is by their—EXAMPLE.

It is very true, as the old proverb says, that—'actions speak louder than words.' If we wish to find out the best way of speaking, we must learn to speak by our example. Let us look at some illustrations of the different ways in which persons have been a blessing to others by their examples.

Our first illustration is about how—

A LITTLE BOY'S EXAMPLE WAS A BLESSING TO HIS FAMILY.

Little Henry was but seven years old. His father was not a Christian. They never had family prayers in their home; nor a blessing asked at their meals. On one occasion a Christian gentleman, who was a friend of Henry's father, was on a visit to their home for several days. During that visit he was invited to conduct family prayers, and to ask a blessing at their meals. It was the first time Henry had ever known this done. He liked it very much, and wished that his father would do so too.

The first evening after this gentleman had left, Henry and his little sister Fannie, and their aged grandmother, sat down to the supper table by themselves, as their father and mother had an engagement out to tea. As they took their seats at the table, Henry said, 'Grandma, may I ask a blessing?'

'Yes,' she replied; and her eyes filled with tears, for she had long been a true Christian.

Henry bowed his head and clasped his little hands together, as he said,—

'God bless our bread and milk; and make us good children. Bless father, and mother, and grandma, for Jesus' sake. Amen.'

Henry went to bed after supper, and thought no more of what he had done. But when his parents came home, late in the evening, the dear old grandma told his father all about it. It touched his father's heart, and filled his eyes with tears. He resolved to take his stand at once, and do his duty to his family. He began, the next day, to have prayers, and ask a blessing at their meals. He soon became an earnest Christian, and joined the Church. Now surely that little boy was a blessing to his father, and his family—by his example.

Our next illustration shows us how—

A LITTLE BOY'S EXAMPLE WAS A BLESSING TO HIS PLAYMATE.

Two boys were playing with their tops one day. Their names were Johnny and Willie. After they had been playing awhile, Johnny got angry, because he could not make his top spin as nicely as Willie's top did, and he began to swear about it.

Willie was very sorry to hear this, and said at once, 'Johnny, if you are going to swear in that way, I can't play with you.'

Johnny replied, very sharply, 'I don't care. You can do as you please; but I'll swear as much as I've a mind to.'

'Well,' said Willie, 'if you're going to keep on swearing, you'll have to do it without me. Good-bye;' and picking up his top he started for home.

When Johnny saw how earnest and decided Willie

was about it, he felt ashamed of himself; and calling after his playmate he said, 'Willie, if you'll come back and play, I won't swear any more.'

Willie went back and said to his playmate, 'Johnny, my Sunday-school teacher says that swearing is very wicked; and I've made up my mind not to play with any boy who will break the third commandment, and take God's name in vain.'

They talked it over awhile, and then Johnny said, 'Well, Willie, I never thought before how wrong it is to swear; but now I am resolved not to swear any more.'

Now Willie was a real hero, to take his stand about this matter so manfully as he did. And we see what a blessing his example was to his friend Johnny.

Our next illustration shows what a blessing came from—

THE EXAMPLE OF A PIOUS CLERK.

This story was told by the late Rev. J. Angel James, who was one of the most useful and successful ministers of the gospel in England during the present century.

'I left home when a young man,' said Mr. James, 'and began my business life as a clerk, in one of the largest business firms in the city of Manchester. I had been religiously educated, but had given up prayer, and cast off the fear of God. I might have gone to utter ruin, if it had not pleased God to make use of the example of a fellow-clerk to save me from destruction. A new clerk had just been taken into the establishment. I knew nothing about him before he came, but was pleased with what I had seen of him the first day that he was in the office. I was requested to let him share my room with me. The first night that he was there, I had gone to bed earlier than usual; but I was not asleep when the new clerk came in. The lamp was burning on the table, and before beginning to undress I noticed that he took out a Bible from his trunk, and sat down to read a chapter. Then he quietly and devoutly kneeled down by the side of his bed, and engaged in silent, earnest prayer. As I lay there and watched him doing this, so quietly, so reverently, my slumbering conscience was roused, and an arrow of deep conviction pierced my heart. I was led to the exercise of true repentance towards God, and of a living faith in my long-neglected Saviour.

'Soon after this,' says Mr. James, 'I gave up business, and began my studies for the ministry. Nearly fifty years have passed away, with all their changes, since this took place; but still, that little chamber—that humble couch—that pious youth bowing down before God in prayer, are as fresh in my memory as though it had occurred but yesterday; and it will never be forgotten, even amidst the glories of the heavenly world, or through all the ages of eternity.'

And if we could only follow that earnest man of God, and see the great good done by his labours, through all the years of his ministry,—what an impressive idea it would give us of the blessing that followed from the silent example of that young man!

I have one other illustration. It shows us the blessing that followed from—

AN AGED CHRISTIAN'S EXAMPLE.

There was a young lady who had great riches, and great beauty; but still was unhappy, because she was a stranger to the peace and hope which Jesus gives to His people. She was not in the habit of visiting the poor; but one day she went with a friend to see a poor old woman, who had been confined to bed for thirty years, who was a very great sufferer, and was near the end of her life. The young lady stood by pitying her; and was surprised to hear not a word of repining, or complaint. The aged Christian only spoke of her happiness and peace, of the many mercies she had experienced, and of the joy and glory that were soon to be hers. How great the contrast was between those two persons! The one had youth, health, and prosperity, and yet was feeling wretched; the other was burdened with age, poverty, and suffering, and yet was perfectly happy. The young lady turned to her friend, and said in a low voice, 'How gladly I would change places with this poor creature, if I could only have the peace and happiness which she is sharing.'

The aged Christian passed away to her home of glorious rest. But her example led that young lady to seek Jesus, and she found in Him the peace and happiness which her youth and wealth could never give. Here we see what a blessing that old Christian was, to that young lady, by her example.

The first way in which God makes His people a blessing is by their *example.*

The second way in which God makes His people a blessing is by their—PRAYERS.

Prayer is the most powerful means of doing good that God has ever put into our hands to use. It has been well said that 'prayer moves the arm that moves the world.' The promise of Jesus to His disciples was, 'All things whatsoever ye shall ask in prayer, believing, ye shall receive' (Matt. xxi. 22). And the Apostle James tells us that 'the effectual fervent prayer of a righteous man availeth much' (James v. 16). Prayer draws down gifts from heaven. It fills the empty soul. It brings strength to the weak, true riches to the poor, and comfort to the sorrowing. It is a bank of wealth; a mine of mercies; a store-house of blessings. It flies where the eagle never flew. It travels farther, and moves faster than the light. Mary, Queen of Scotland, understood the power of prayer when she used to say, 'I am more afraid of John Knox's prayers, than of an army of ten thousand men.' It is very true, as the hymn says, that—

'Prayer makes the darkened cloud withdraw;
Prayer climbs the ladder Jacob saw,—
Gives exercise to faith and love,—
Brings every blessing from above.'

The Bible is full of illustrations of the good that has been done, or the blessings that have been secured, by prayer. Let us look at just two of these.

See, there are the children of Israel going out of Egypt. They have not gone far, before Pharaoh, king of Egypt, goes after them, with an army, to bring them back. Look at their situation when Pharaoh overtakes them. They are going along a road on the shore of the Red Sea. A range of high mountains rises up on their right hand, while on their left hand, the sea spreads out its broad waters. What are they to do? It seems impossible for them to escape. But Moses, their great leader, had faith in the power of prayer. All that he could do was to pray to God for help. He did pray. And God heard his prayer, and sent the needed help. God opened a way for them through the depths of the sea. He stretched out His Almighty arm, and piled up the water like walls of glass, on each side of them. They marched in safety, by the way thus opened for them, through the depths of the sea. The Egyptians attempted to follow them by the same path. But, just as they reached the middle of the sea, the piled-up waters rushed down upon them, and they were drowned. What a blessing that was to the

Israelites! It delivered them from their enemies, and saved them from being led back as captives to Egypt. But this blessing came to them in answer to the prayer of Moses.

And here is another illustration of the power of prayer, in the history of the Israelites. It occurs at the time when Elijah the Tishbite is God's prophet to the people. A long drought has been sent upon them, as a punishment for their sins. For three years and six months there has not been a drop of rain in the land. The springs have failed. The streams have dried up. The fields are parched. The crops have perished. The trees are withering. The horses and cattle are dying, and desolation and death are threatening ruin to the nation. What can the prophet do? He engages in prayer, that God would send rain upon the earth. Long and earnestly he continues his petitions. While he is thus engaged, a little cloud, about as big as a man's hand, is seen, rising out of the sea. It grows larger and larger. Presently the heavens are black with clouds, and the rain pours down in torrents, refreshing the parched earth, filling the exhausted springs and streams, and restoring the long-lost beauty and fertility of the fields and the forests. What a blessing that rain was to the nation of Israel! And it was the prayer of the prophet Elijah which brought down that great blessing upon them.

And now, let us look at some illustrations, outside of the Bible, of the power which prayer exerts in bringing down blessings.

Our first illustration may be called—

THE LOST SHEEP FOUND BY PRAYER.

Many years ago a little boy, named Jacob, was bound out at an early age to a Scotch farmer, that he might learn farming as his life work. His father was a good Christian man. He had instructed him in religion; and especially had taught him to pray, when he was in any trouble, and to ask help from God.

One afternoon Jakie was sent over the hills, to fetch the sheep home before dark. He had often been sent on this errand before, and had never met with any difficulty in finding them. But on this occasion, when he got to the usual place for them, they were not to be seen. He searched all around, but in vain. The sheep were lost. What should he do? He remembered what his father had taught him about prayer; and felt that now was the time for him to seek in this way the help that he needed, and knew not how else to get. So he kneeled down, closed his eyes, folded his hands, and said: 'Now, Lord, I am a poor little boy. They have sent me here to fetch the sheep home; but I cannot find them. They are lost. Lord, thou knowest where they are. Please help me to find the sheep, for Jesus' sake. Amen.' He remained on his knees for some time after finishing his prayer with his eyes shut, feeling very happy to think that he had a friend always near to help him. While waiting thus, he heard the distant bleating of a sheep. Rising to his feet, he started in the direction from which the sound came, and soon found the sheep, all together in a little out-of-the-way valley, which he had never seen before. Then he drove the sheep home, thinking to himself as he went along—what a blessing prayer is!

Here is another illustration. We may call it—

A LIAR CURED BY PRAYER.

A poor widow woman in England, who supported herself by sewing, had a little boy named Charley. He was disobedient and careless; would use bad words, and tell stories. He gave his mother a great deal of trouble. She tried all she could to make him better; but it was no use. He went on getting worse and worse. Finally she concluded to send him to the parish school, connected with the church to which she belonged.

He behaved very badly in this school; and had not been there long before he was found guilty of saying something that was very untrue.

The clergyman of the parish was greatly troubled about him. He came into the school to see what was to be done in the case. He called Charley out, and placed him in a chair in the middle of the school. Then he spoke to the scholars about the evil of lying; and asked them what they thought should be done to Charley, to break him off this bad habit, and make a good boy of him.

'Oh, sir!' said one little boy, 'suppose we put him in the corner.'

Another boy said, 'Oh, sir, suppose we give him a good whipping.'

A third little boy said, 'Suppose, sir, we *pray* for him.'

'Ah! my little boy,' said the minister, 'you are right. He has been whipped, and put in the corner; but he is none the better. But we have not *prayed* for him yet. Let us do this now.'

Then they all knelt down, and the minister offered up an earnest prayer. He asked God to pardon Charley's sin; to show him the great evil of lying; and to give him grace to break off from this bad habit, and to resolve always to speak the truth.

Charley was very much affected by that prayer. When they rose from their knees, his cheeks were wet with tears. A change took place in him from that day. He soon became one of the best boys in the school, and was never known, after that, to tell a lie. What a blessing followed from that prayer!

I have one more story, under this part of our sermon. It shows us how—

A DRUNKARD WAS SAVED BY THE PRAYER OF HIS CHILD.

An intemperate man, who had once been well off, but had wasted his property by drink, returned to his home one night, earlier than usual, and not so much under the influence of liquor. He took a chair, in a distant corner of the room, in which his wife and daughter were sitting. The little one was only four years old. There was no carpet on the floor of that room, and most of its furniture had been pawned for food. His conscience was troubling him, and he was very unhappy as he sat there. 'Come, my darling,' said the mother to her child, 'it's time to go to bed.' Then the little one knelt down by her mother's side, to say her prayers. And as she looked up into that loving face, and saw the deep marks of sorrow on it, her young heart was melted. She finished her prayers as usual; and then, without rising from her knees, she said, 'Mamma, dear, may I say one more prayer?'

'Yes, my darling, pray on.' Then, with her eyes closed, she lifted up her tiny hands and said, 'O God! spare, oh! spare my dear papa, and make him a good Christian, for Jesus' sake. Amen.'

Her Father in heaven heard that prayer, and so did her father on earth. The word 'Amen!' burst from that father's lips. And then, with the tears of penitence streaming down his cheeks, he clasped the mother and her little one to his bosom. 'My child!' said he, 'you have saved your father from a drunkard's grave. I'll sign the pledge to-night.'

He did so; and drank no more after that. What a blessing followed from that dear child's prayer!

The second way in which God makes His people a blessing is by their *prayers.*

The third way in which God makes His people a blessing is by their—WORK.

This means by what they do to show their love to Him. When Jesus was on earth we are told that—'He went about *doing good.*' He was the greatest blessing our world ever saw. And all His people are expected to follow His example; and, as one of our beautiful Collects says—'to tread in the blessed steps of His most holy life.' True, Jesus had the power of working miracles. He could open the eyes of the blind; and unstop the ears of the deaf; and heal the sick, and give relief to all sorts of sufferers. We cannot do the miracles which Jesus did. But still we can follow His example, and 'go about doing good,' as He did, in other ways. We can give food to the hungry, and clothes to the naked, and show kindness and sympathy to those who are in trouble. And in this way, every follower of Jesus may be a blessing wherever he goes.

There is no more beautiful illustration, of the way in which any Christian may be a blessing, than is found in the book of Job. This is the oldest book in the Bible. Job is supposed to have lived in the time of Abraham. And in the twenty-ninth chapter of this book, we have an interesting account given of the way in which Job made himself a blessing to those about him.

He says—'When the ear heard me, then it blessed me; and when the eye saw me, it gave witness to me: because I delivered the poor that cried, the fatherless, and him that hath none to help him. The blessing of him that was ready to perish came upon me; and I caused the widow's heart to sing for joy. I was eyes to the blind, and feet was I to the lame. I was a father to the poor: and the cause which I knew not, I searched out.'

Here we see how Job made himself a blessing; and if we follow his example, we shall be blessings too. Let us look at some illustrations of the different ways in which Christians may be blessings. The first may be called—

MAKING PEOPLE HAPPY.

The Rev. Sydney Smith, a well-known clergyman in England, cut a little article from the paper one day, about making people happy, and made up his mind to try and practise it. This was it—'When you rise in the morning, say to yourself, "I will try to do good to somebody to-day. If I meet with a hungry man, I will get him something to eat. If I meet one suffering from the cold, I will get him some extra clothing. If I meet with some one in trouble, by a kind look, or a kind word, I will try to comfort him."'

How easy it would be to do this! If we do this every day; then, at the end of the year, it will be a comfort to think, that while that year was going by, we have been a comfort and blessing to three hundred and sixty-five persons. And if we keep on doing this for forty years, then it will have been our privilege to have been a blessing to fourteen thousand six hundred people.

Our next story shows us—

HOW A LITTLE GIRL WAS A BLESSING.

A gentleman in England was walking up and down the room, at a railway station, waiting for a train. He held by the hand his little daughter, a lovely child about five or six years old. As they were waiting there, two policemen came in, bringing with them a prisoner in chains. He was a very wicked man. For something very wrong, which he had lately done, he had just been sentenced to the penitentiary for twenty years. The policemen were taking him to the prison. They gave him a seat in a corner of the room. He was a savage, sullen looking man. As the gentleman walked up and down the room, his little girl could not keep her eyes off the poor prisoner. At first she was afraid of him; but after a while this feeling changed to pity. And once, when they reached that part of the room where he was, she let go her father's hand, and, coming up to the prisoner, in a gentle voice, and with her eyes full of tears, she said, 'Man, I am sorry for you.' But he frowned at her fiercely, and she ran back to her father's side.

They continued their walk, and after a while, when they came near him again, she loosed her father's hand, and going towards him, she said in the same tender, pitying tones, 'Man, the Lord Jesus is sorry for you too.'

Then the train came, and they all went off. When the policemen reached the end of their journey, they delivered their prisoner to the keeper of the prison. After doing this, they told him they were sorry for what they had to say about this prisoner. 'He is ill-tempered, and disobedient, and very hard to manage; and we are afraid he will occasion you great trouble.' This made the keeper of the prison feel very uncomfortable. For he had so many troublesome cases already on hand, that he did not want to have another. But to his surprise he found no trouble with this man. He did whatever he was told to do, and was always respectful and pleasant in his manner. He could not tell what to make of it. So after a while he spoke to him on the subject, and asked how it was that he was so different from what had been reported.

'Why, sir,' said the prisoner, 'that report was true. I used to be as bad as possible. But now I am a changed man.' Then he went on to tell about what that dear child had said to him, while waiting in the railway station. 'Her sweet words melted my hard heart,' said he. 'They reminded me of my sainted mother, now in heaven. They led me to see what a sinner I was. I turned in penitence to Jesus. He heard my prayers. He gave me His pardon and peace. Now I am a new man; and am ready to meet my dear mother in heaven, whenever God's time for the change shall come.'

What a blessing that dear child was to that poor prisoner!

HOW A NEW YORK GENTLEMAN WAS A BLESSING.

This gentleman was an earnest Christian. He often spent a part of Sunday afternoon, in trying to do good among the people he would find idling away their time on the wharves. One Sunday he met a man there who was known to be a great rogue. He had been in the penitentiary for stealing.

The gentleman went up to him, and laying his hand kindly on his shoulder, said, 'My friend, do you love the Lord Jesus Christ?'

The man turned rudely round, and said: 'You're a pretty fellow to talk to me in this way. It's the way you Christians do. I'd like to see you put your religion in practice.'

It was a cold day, and the man was thinly dressed and shivering. The gentleman had two coats on.

'Show me your religion,' said the man, 'by giving me one of your coats.'

In a moment the gentleman took off one of his coats,

and threw it round the man's shoulders. He was astonished, and taking off the coat said,—

'I was only joking. I wanted to see how far your religion would carry you. I believe you are a real Christian. What do you want me to do?'

'Ah! my friend,' said the gentleman, 'I want you to come to Jesus; and to go with me to our meeting this afternoon. Will you?'

'Yes, I will,' said the man. The gentleman took him to church with him. He engaged him to come again, and the end of it was, that man became an earnest Christian, and was very useful in labouring among the sailors.

Surely that Christian gentleman was a blessing by the work he did that day.

Now where is our text to-day? Gen. xii. 2. What are the words of the text? 'Thou shalt be a blessing.' What is the sermon about? How Christians are a blessing. We have spoken of how many ways in which they are so? Three. In the *first place* God makes His people a blessing, by what? By their *example.* In the *second* by what? By their *prayers.* And in the *third* by what? By their *work.*

Let us all try to love and serve the Lord Jesus, and then He will help us to be blessings in these and other ways, wherever we go.

VIII.

THE PROMISED REFUGE.

'*The eternal God is thy refuge.*'—DEUT. xxxiii. 27.

HERE we have another of the precious promises of God's holy word. When we are young and anything troubles us, we always run to our dear mother, and find refuge in her loving arms. But when our mother dies; or when we grow up, and go away from home, we are not able to use *that* refuge any longer. And yet, we always need a refuge, wherever we may go. There are trials and troubles that must meet us, on the right hand and the left; and when these troubles come upon us, they will make us very unhappy, unless we have a refuge to which we can go, with the burden of our trials, and in which we can find the help and comfort that we need. And it was just because God knew about the trials that await us, and how much we should need a refuge in meeting them, that He has given us the blessed promise that we have in our text. Here He teaches us to think of Himself—'the eternal God'—as our refuge.

Our sermon to-day is about—*the promised refuge.*

And in speaking about it, the question we have to try and answer is—what sort of a refuge is this? There are *four* things about this refuge to speak of. These will show us that it is just the kind of refuge that we need; and the very best that can be found.

The first thing to speak of, about this refuge, is that it is—NEAR.

Our earthly refuges are always confined to one particular place. Sometimes the refuge that we need is very far off, and when danger threatens us, or trouble overtakes us, we cannot reach the refuge in time; and then, it is of no use to us.

Among the Jews, if one person killed another by accident, without intending to do it, the father, or son, or brother, or nearest relative of the dead man, was called 'the avenger of blood.' The law of custom was, that this person should go after the one who had caused the death of his relative, and kill him at once, without waiting for a trial by judge and jury, as is the custom with us. But, for the protection of those who had by accident caused the death of others, God appointed what were called—'cities of refuge'—in different parts of the land. To any one of those cities the man-slayer, who had killed a person without intending it, might flee for refuge, and if he could get there before the avenger of blood overtook him, he would be safe. But those cities of refuge were not always near. Sometimes the nearest of them would be so far off, that a man would have to run for half a day before he could reach it. And while he was trying to get there, he might be overtaken, and killed.

But how different it is with the refuge we are considering! *God* forms this refuge. And He is always present, everywhere. As the Bible says—'He is a God *at hand*, and not afar off.' We can get away from our homes, and from our friends, but we never can get away from God. How beautifully David brings out this idea in the 139th Psalm (7–10), when he says: 'Whither shall I go from Thy spirit? or whither shall I flee from Thy presence? If I ascend up into heaven, Thou art there; if I make my bed in hell, behold, Thou art there. If I take the wings of the morning, and dwell in the uttermost parts of the sea; even there shall Thy hand lead me, and Thy right hand shall hold me.'

This is a blessed refuge because it is always near. We never have to go far to find it. Here are some illustrations of this part of our subject.

A teacher once asked this question of his scholars, 'Boys, where is God?' One boy answered, 'God is in heaven.' Another said, 'God is everywhere;' and another said, 'God is *here*.' And this is true, not in *one* place only, but in every place. He is always near to everybody.

HOW A LITTLE BOY FELT GOD NEAR.

This little fellow had been lost in one of the dense forests of the West. He had to stay all night in the woods. The next day he was found and taken home. His mother, in talking to him about it, asked him 'if he was not afraid? and what he did when night came on?'

'No, mamma,' said the little fellow—'I was not afraid; because I knew that God was there. So when it got dark I kneeled down and said: "O God! I have lost my way, and cannot get home, but have to stay here all night in the woods. O God, please take care of little Johnny; and don't let anything hurt me; for Jesus' sake. Amen." Then I lay down and went to sleep.'

This was a beautiful illustration of David's words when he says, 'The angel of the Lord encampeth round them that fear Him, and delivereth them' (Ps. xxxiv. 7). That little boy was feeling that God was a *near* refuge. He turned to that refuge, in the loneliness of the woods, and amidst the darkness of the night; and he found there just the protection and the safety that he needed.

I have only one other illustration for this part of our subject. We may call it—

HELP BY A RAVEN.

A good many years ago, in a village near Warsaw, in Poland, there lived a pious peasant by the name of Dobry. He was an honest, industrious man, but very poor. He had been sick, and not able to work for some weeks. In consequence of this he got behindhand with his rent, and was unable to pay it. His landlord was a very hard man. He had called several times for the money, but could not get it. This made him angry, and he told Dobry that unless the rent was paid before the close of that day, he would send a constable the next morning, and have him turned out of doors. This distressed the poor man very much. For it was just in the midst of winter. The weather was very severe. They had several small children; and the idea of being all turned out into the cold, when they had no place to go to for shelter, was dreadful. But Dobry was a Christian man. He knew that 'the eternal God was the refuge' of His people. He knew what a near refuge this is. He had often turned to this refuge before, when he was in trouble, and had always found relief there. He resolved to do so again, in his present trouble. So, at the close of the day, he gathered his family together for their evening prayer. Before engaging in prayer he read the 50th Psalm, in which this precious promise is found: 'Call upon Me in the day of trouble, and I will deliver thee.'

Then they kneeled in prayer. Dobry told the Lord of their present trouble, and asked Him to please not let them be turned out of their home, in the midst of winter. When the prayer was over, they sat down again, and sang one of their favourite hymns. The hymn they sang that evening was one of which this is the first verse—

'Commit thou all thy griefs
And ways into His hands,
To His sure trust and tender care,
Who heaven and earth commands.'

The last verse of this hymn reads thus—

'Thou on the Lord rely,
So safe shalt thou go on;
Fix on His word thy stedfast eye,
So shall thy work be done.'

While they were singing this verse, there was a pecking at the door. Dobry opened the door and a raven came in. This was an old friend of theirs. Dobry's father had taken it out of the nest when it was quite young. He had nursed it very kindly, and tamed it, and then let it go. But the bird never seemed to forget the kindness that had been shown to him, and he often came into their house, as though it was his home. As he hopped into the house, on this occasion, Dobry saw that the raven had something in his bill. He reached out his hand to receive it, and the bird laid down on the palm of his hand a gold ring, set with precious jewels.

Dobry felt very thankful when he saw this. He knew that his Father in heaven had sent it. He took it immediately to his minister to show it to him, and ask him what he should do with it. On looking at it he saw that it belonged to Stanislaus, the king of Poland. Then he took it to him, and told him the story connected with it. The king was greatly interested in the story. He sent for Dobry, and rewarded him liberally, so that he was no longer in need. Then he built him a new house, and gave him a nice little farm, which he supplied with cattle from his own herd. Over the door of the house, a stone tablet was put in; and on the tablet was engraved a raven with a ring in his beak; and under it, the promise which had been so wonderfully fulfilled on that occasion: 'Call upon Me in the day of trouble, and I will deliver thee' (Ps. l. 15).

Now surely that poor man found 'the eternal God' a refuge *near* to him in trouble. The first thing to speak of, about this refuge, is that it is a near refuge.

The second thing about it, to speak of, is that it is—A LARGE—*refuge.*

Some refuges are small in their size. They can only hold a certain number of persons. They often get filled up, and no matter how many people may apply for entrance, they cannot get in. Some refuges are only open on certain days, or at certain hours of the day. If persons apply for entrance on other days, or at other hours of the day, they find the doors closed, and they cannot get in.

But this is never the case with the refuge we are considering. This is so large that, no matter how many people press into it, there is always room for as many more. The gracious invitation which Jesus, who forms this refuge, gives is—'Come unto Me, *all* ye who labour and are heavy laden, and I will give you rest.' And then, in another place, the invitation that comes to us from this glorious refuge is in this form: 'The Spirit and the bride say, Come; let him that heareth say, Come; let him that is athirst come; and *whosoever will*, let him come, and take of the water of life freely.'

And this invitation is not only to all persons but at *lla, times.* The gates of this refuge rae never closed. By day or by night, in summer and in winter, any persons, who desire to do so, may come and enter. Then how large this refuge must be! Yes, it *is* large. Our text tells us that it is—'The *eternal* God' who forms this refuge. But God is called *infinite*, as well as eternal. This word infinite is a big word. If you look into your

JAMES SIMPSON.

dictionary to find out its meaning, you will see that it means something which has no limits, or bounds. We know many large things. But they are not infinite. They have their limits, or their bounds. The ocean is large, but it is not infinite. It has a bottom, and it has shores; and these form the limits, or bounds of the ocean. Our world is large; yet it is not infinite. It has a north, and a south, and an east, and a west; and these form the limits, or bounds of the world. But God is an infinite God, because there are no limits, and no bounds to Him. He is present *all the time, everywhere.* And the refuge which He forms must be just as large as He is Himself. It is a refuge always *near*, because God, who forms it, is in every place, at all times; and it is a refuge which has no limits, or bounds, and therefore must be so large, that it never can be filled. No matter how many flee unto this refuge, it is never full.

Let us look at some illustrations of this part of our subject. Our first story is about the word—*Whosoever.*

James Simpson was an English weaver, a man in very humble circumstances. He had become very much interested in the subject of religion, and was anxious to find the Saviour. But he had never had any instruction on this important matter, and was all in the dark about it. He was thinking of it all the time; and the great question that was always before him was, 'What must I do to be saved?'

One evening, after the day's work was over, he was sitting by the window in their little cottage, with the New Testament before him, trying to read it. He knew very little about reading, and had to spell out each word as he came to it. He was trying to read the seventeenth verse of the twenty-second chapter of Revelation, and was spelling his way along, when he came to a word with which he began thus: 'w-h-o, who—s-o, whoso—e-v-e-r, whosoever; ay, but that's a big word,' said he. 'I wonder what it means?' Then he spelled out the rest of the verse and read it: 'Whosoever will, let him come and take of the water of life freely.'

'I remember,' he thought to himself, 'the minister said that "the water of life" here means salvation. But what does this big word "whosoever" mean? If I could only find this out,' he said to himself, 'how glad I should be!' After thinking over it awhile, he rose, and put his hat on, and with his Testament under his arm, he went out to take a walk.

There was a large boarding-school for boys in that neighbourhood, and the thought occurred to him, that one of the scholars from this school could tell him the meaning of this big word which he could not understand. So he walked towards the school, and just as he reached the gate, a bright, good-natured looking boy, about fifteen years of age, came out to catch the ball, with which he and his companions were playing.

James went up to him, and said, 'I say, young master, may I speak a word with you?'

'You can speak two or three, if you please, sir,' said the boy very pleasantly, 'only be quick about it, as my companions are waiting for me.'

'I thought that maybe you'd tell me what these letters mean, when put together,' said James, spelling out the big word which had puzzled him so much. Then he put the Testament into the boy's hand, pointing out the verse in which the big word was found.

'That's "whosoever,"' said the boy.

'And pray, sir,' asked James, anxiously, 'will you please tell me what "whosoever" means?'

The boy looked at the word for a moment, and then said, 'Why, sir, it means *you*, or *me*, or *anybody*.'

'Thank you kindly, sir,' said the poor man, 'you've

done me a great favour. I am very much obliged to you.'

The boy hurried on to join his companions, and James returned to his home, saying to himself—' "You, or me, or anybody." Then there is salvation for me. The refuge is large enough to take me in.'

Our next illustration may be called—

JERUSALEM SINNERS.

This was used by John Bunyan, the author of *Pilgrim's Progress.* He was trying to show how large the refuge is which the gospel offers for the salvation of men. And in doing this, he quoted the words which the Apostle Peter used, in the sermon he preached to the Jews, at Jerusalem, after our Saviour had gone back to heaven. 'Then said Peter unto them, Repent, and be baptized *every one of you* in the name of Jesus Christ for the remission of sins.' Then Bunyan represents different persons as coming to Peter and asking if it was possible for them to be saved.

One man came and said, 'I was among those who plotted to take away the life of Christ. Is it possible that *I* can be saved?'

Peter's answer was, '*Every one* of you.'

'But I was one of those who bare false witness against Him. Is there any hope for me?'

'For every one of you,' said Peter.

'But I was one of those that cried out, "Crucify Him! crucify Him!" Can there be any pardon for me?'

'I am sent,' said Peter, 'to preach repentance, and remission of sins to—*every one* of you.'

'But I was one of them that did spit in His face, when He stood before His accusers. I was also one that mocked Him, when He hung in anguish, bleeding on the tree. Is there room for me?'

'For *every one of you,*' said Peter.

'But I was one of those who railed on Him,' said another. 'I reviled Him. I hated Him. Can there be any hope for me?'

'There is,' said Peter, 'for every one of you.'

Oh, what a blessing there is in these words,—'every one of you.' Here we see how large the refuge is which we find in Jesus! No matter how many enter it, there is always room for more. It is a *large* refuge.

In the third place it is—A WELL-FURNISHED—*refuge.*

In this world, it sometimes happens, that people reach a refuge they have been seeking, and enter it; but they do not find in it what they need. They may be very hungry when they enter the refuge; but they do not find in it the food they need to satisfy their hunger. They may be very thirsty; but there is no water in the refuge for them to drink. They may be almost naked; yet find no clothes in the refuge for them to wear, to keep them warm and comfortable. They may be suffering from some painful disease; but there is no medicine in the refuge that will heal their disease, and relieve their sufferings.

Now, under these circumstances the refuge would be of little use. We might as well be out of it as in it. It is not a well-furnished refuge. It would do us but little good to be in it.

But ah! how different it is with that refuge for our souls, that we find in Jesus—the eternal God! All who enter this refuge find that it is indeed a well-furnished refuge. If our souls are hungry as we enter it, we find here 'the bread that came down from heaven;' and this relieves our hunger. If our souls are thirsty, we find here 'the water of life,' and this satisfies our thirst. If our souls need clothing, we find here 'the garments of salvation,'—the glorious 'robes of righteousness' which Jesus has prepared for His people to wear. If our souls are suffering from any spiritual disease, we can find in this refuge 'the balm of Gilead'—which will heal them, and make them well. If we feel that our souls are poor, when we enter this refuge, we can find here the gold and the silver, the gems and the jewels of the heavenly world, and these will make us truly rich. And so all our wants will be supplied. Everything that our souls can need, to make them happy for ever, can be found in this refuge. And so we may well speak of it as a well-furnished refuge.

John Newton was feeling how well this refuge is furnished, when he wrote the hymn we often sing—

> 'How sweet the name of Jesus sounds,
> In a believer's ear!
> It soothes his sorrows, heals his wounds,
> And drives away his fear.
>
> 'It makes the wounded spirit whole,
> And calms the troubled breast;
> 'Tis manna to the hungry soul,
> And to the weary rest.'

And Dr. Doddridge was having the same view of this refuge, when he wrote that beautiful hymn—

> 'Jesus! I love Thy charming name,
> 'Tis music to mine ear;
> Fain would I sound it out so loud,
> That earth and heaven might hear.
>
> 'Yes!—Thou art precious to my soul,
> My transport and my trust;
> Jewels, to Thee, are gaudy toys,
> And gold is sordid dust.

'All my capacious powers can wish,
In Thee doth richly meet;
Not to mine eyes is light so dear,
Nor friendship half so sweet.'

I have just one story to show the meaning of this part of our subject, or how well-furnished this refuge is. We may call it—

WHAT AN OLD SLAVE FOUND IN THIS REFUGE.

Twenty-five or thirty years ago, a New York merchant, was travelling through Virginia. He was a Christian man, and always carried his religion with him. On this occasion he had lost his way; so he stopped at a little cabin, by the roadside, to try and get some information about it. He knocked at the door of the cabin, and an old negro came to see who was there. He had been a slave all his days, but was now too old to work any more, and he lived in that old cabin alone by himself. The gentleman asked him some questions about the road he had to travel, and soon got all the information that he desired. Then he went into the little cabin, and sat down to have a talk with the old negro. He asked him a number of questions, about his past life, which were answered satisfactorily. Then, as he looked round the cabin in which he was sitting, he saw that there was nothing in it but an old bed, a little broken table, and a few broken chairs. It was winter, and the cabin was cold and smoky. 'My friend,' said the traveller, 'your cabin has so little in it to make you comfortable, I don't see how you manage to get along all by yourself. Don't you feel very lonely and sad here?'

'Oh no,' said the old man; 'I never feel lonely, or sad. I have known and loved the blessed Saviour for many years. He lives with me, and that makes it always pleasant here. He pardons all my sins. He supplies all my wants. I find everything I need in Him. The thought of Jesus makes me happy by day and by night.'

Now, surely, that poor old slave found this refuge, which Jesus makes for His people—*a well-furnished* refuge.

The fourth and last thing that we would say about this refuge is, that it is—A SAFE—*refuge.*

It is very important for us to know that this refuge is safe. The other good things about it, of which we have spoken, will be of little consequence unless we can be sure that, when we enter this refuge, we shall find ourselves safe in it. No matter how near it may be—nor how large—nor how well-furnished; it will all be of no use unless at the same time it is safe. We may find all the good things in it that we need, and yet, unless we can be sure that this refuge cannot be destroyed, or that our enemies cannot follow us there to do us harm, it would be good for nothing after all.

Whatever earthly refuges we may flee to, it never can be said of them that they are perfectly safe. Some enemy may follow us there, and be powerful enough to burst open the iron gates of the refuge, or to break down its stone walls; and then we should be in the power of our enemy, and he could do us all the harm he pleased.

But it is very different with the refuge which we find in our eternal God. The safety of this refuge does not depend on locks, or bolts, or bars—on gates of brass, or walls of stone. God Himself forms this refuge. This makes its safety perfect. His almighty power is exercised, all the time, for the safety of those who enter this refuge. And unless some one can be found whose power and wisdom are greater than God's, those who enter this refuge never need fear about its safety. God watches over it night and day. His unslumbering eye is ever upon it. His outspread wing is ever over it; and His almighty arm is ever around it. And so, when we enter this refuge, we may do it with the assurance that we are perfectly safe within its walls.

Here are some illustrations of the safety found in this refuge, and of the comfort which we should find in the thought of this safety.

Our first story may be called—

PAPA IS RUNNING THE ENGINE.

'Some years ago,' says a Christian gentleman, 'I was in a train of cars, on the Baltimore and Ohio Railway. The train was behind time, and was rushing along at an unusually rapid rate. The passengers were afraid that some accident would happen, and all eyes were turned anxiously to the windows, as the train flew past.

'I was thinking of the fearful scenes that would be witnessed, if the train should be thrown over the embankment, when I saw a bright little girl, four or five years old, coming towards me. She held out her little hand, and said, "Good morning," in a sweet clear voice. I asked her if she was not afraid to ride in the cars.

'"*Sometimes* I am. But this morning I am not at all afraid." "Why," I asked, "are you not afraid this morning? Everybody else seems to be afraid, because we are running so rapidly." "Oh, there is no danger at all to-day," she replied, "because father is running the engine."'

Her father was the engineer, and she had such entire confidence in his ability to protect her, that she felt perfectly safe and happy. And if that dear child could have such confidence in her earthly father, how much more we should trust in our heavenly Father, who is 'running the engine' of this world's government; and is ordering and controlling everything in heaven above, and upon the earth beneath! When clouds, and storms, and darkness surround our path, let us think of our Father in heaven, and feel safe, in all dangers, because He is our refuge, and nothing can harm us while under His care.

Our next story is about—

THE COMFORT FOUND FROM TRUSTING GOD.

During an earthquake that took place a few years ago, the inhabitants of a small village were very much alarmed. But there was a good old Christian lady who lived there, and whom all the villagers knew very well. They were very much surprised to see how calm and happy this old lady was, when all the rest of the villagers were so very much frightened.

At last one of her friends said to her, 'Why, mother, how is it that you are not afraid when the earth is shaking so?'

'I am not afraid,' was her answer, 'because I know I have a God who can shake the world; and who is able to keep me perfectly safe while winds are blowing, or storms are bursting, or earthquakes are rending the ground.'

That good old Christian was in this refuge, and we see how safe it made her feel!

I have only one other story. It may be called—

OUR SAFETY IN CHRIST.

'When I was in England,' says a good Christian lady from Philadelphia, 'a friend told me a simple story in which I was greatly interested. The reason why I was so pleased with this story, was because it illustrates so beautifully the safety we find, when we flee to Jesus as our refuge.

'"I was taking a nap one summer afternoon," said my friend, "while staying at the home of my aunt in the country. Presently I was wakened by hearing a strange sort of noise, as if something was knocking at the window. I rose, and went to the window, to find out what it was. When I got there I found a butterfly, inside the window-pane, in a great fright. He saw a large sparrow, standing on the window ledge, outside, pecking at the window, and trying to get in. The butterfly did not see the glass, nor know that it was there. But it knew that the sparrow was its enemy and it was afraid, every minute, that the sparrow would catch it and eat it up. Poor thing! no wonder it was afraid. And the sparrow did not see the glass either. It was expecting every minute to get hold of the butterfly, and make a good dinner of it. And yet the poor butterfly was just as safe as if it had been miles and miles away. That thick pane of glass was between it and its enemy; and that made a safe refuge for it."'

And so it is with us when we come to Jesus as our refuge, and abide in Him. We are safe then, perfectly safe. His presence, and His power, are between us and every danger. He says to us, as He said to Abraham, 'Fear not; I am thy shield.' This shield is what makes our refuge safe.

Let us remember the four things about this refuge of which we have spoken. It is a *near* refuge; a *large* refuge; *a well-furnished* refuge; and a *safe* refuge. Let us thank God for providing such a refuge for us. Let us all flee to this refuge, and abide in it; and then, in life, and in death—in time, and in eternity—it will be well with us.

'*The eternal God is thy refuge.*'

IX.

THE PROMISE OF THE DEW.

'*I will be as the dew unto Israel.*'—HOSEA xiv. 5.

THIS is a beautiful promise. It was first made to the Jews; but it belongs just as truly to us Gentiles, when we become Christians, as it did to the Jews. We can take it as our own. And we may learn from it some very useful, practical lessons. Here God promises to be to us 'as the dew.' We all know what the dew is. If we are out in the country, and take a walk in the morning before breakfast, we shall see, on the flowers in the garden, and on the grass in the fields, tiny little drops of water, clear as crystal, and sparkling with beauty as the sunbeams fall upon them. Those are drops of dew. They are just like so many bright jewels, or little rainbows. And if you ask where those dewdrops come from, it is easy to answer the question.

You know there is always more or less of moisture in the air around us. As the sun shines on the ponds, or lakes, or streams about us, it makes the water on the surface warm. Then some of it turns into vapour, and floats away in the atmosphere. But when night comes on, the air gets cooler; and then it has to give up some of the moisture which it had received during the day. And so it leaves this moisture in the drops of dew, that are formed on the flowers, and on the grass.

Somebody has well said, that—'the drops of dew are the tears which night sheds for the absence of the sun.'

The dew is very useful in all countries. But it was particularly so in the land of Israel. They did not have much rain there. But they had heavier dews than we have in our country. The flowers in the gardens of the Israelites, and the grass in their fields, would all have withered and died if it had not been for the abundant dew they had. It was a great blessing to them. And when God promises, in our text, to be 'as the dew' to His people, He means to say that the blessing of His grace shall do good to our souls, just as the dew does to the flowers and the grass. And so, our sermon to-day is about—*the promise of the dew.*

The plants in our gardens receive *three* blessings, from the dew which falls upon them; and the dew of God's grace brings the same blessings to our souls.

The first blessing which follows from the dew is—LIFE AND GROWTH.

The grass of the field, and the flowers of the garden, depend on the dew to keep them alive, and to help them to grow. But the dew of God's blessing does more for our souls, than the natural dew can do for the flowers of the field. If the flowers are dead, all the natural dew in the world never could make one of them alive again. But the dew of God's grace or blessing can do this. It is making dead souls alive all the time. And then it keeps them alive, and makes them grow. This was what the apostle meant when he said, 'By the grace of God I am what I am.' It was the grace of God, or the dew of His blessing, which changed him from being a persecutor of the Church of God, to be a Christian, and a preacher of that gospel which he had once laboured hard to destroy. And it was the same dew of God's blessing which made him so earnest and faithful in seeking to spread abroad the knowledge of Christ, and His salvation, to the ends of the earth.

Now, let us look at some illustrations of the way in which the dew of God's blessing causes the souls of His people to grow in what is good. Our first story shows—

HOW A GENTLE BOY GREW TO BE A GENTLEMAN.

'You see I am a gentleman!' said Will Thompson. 'I will take no insult.' And the little fellow strutted up and down in a rage. He had been throwing stones at Peter Jones, and he thought that his anger proved him to be a gentleman.

'If you want to be a gentleman,' said his teacher, who was standing by, 'I should think you would be a gentle boy first. Gentlemen do not throw stones at their neighbours. Peter Jones did not throw stones at you, and I think he is much more likely to prove a gentleman.'

'But he's got patches on his pantaloons,' said Will, in a scornful tone.

'Bad pantaloons don't keep a boy from being a gentleman,' said the teacher, 'but a bad temper does. Now, William, if you want to be a gentleman, you must first be a gentle boy.'

After walking farther on, the teacher met little Peter Jones. Some stones had hit him, and he was hurt by them.

'Well, Peter, what's the matter between you and Will this morning?' asked the teacher.

'I was throwing a ball at one of the boys in play, sir, and it missed him, and hit Will Thompson's dog.'

'Why did you not throw back at him, when he had thrown at you?'

'Because, sir, my mother says if I want to be a gentleman, I must learn to be a gentle boy; so I thought it was best to keep out of his way, till he had time to cool down a little.'

The teacher praised Peter for the way in which he had acted, and encouraged him to go on doing so. Then, as he walked towards his home, he made up his mind to watch those two boys and see how they turned out. He lived to see them both grow up. Will Thompson turned out to be a selfish, rowdy fellow, whom nobody loved, or cared for; while Peter Jones became a gentleman who was loved and respected by all who knew him.

But it was the dew of God's blessing resting on that gentle boy, which caused him to grow up into the gentleman that he afterwards became.

Our next illustration may be called—

THE COLOURED MAN AND THE BIBLE.

The tree is known by its fruits, and a book is known by its effects. An infidel once told a coloured Christian man, that the Bible, of which he loved to talk so much, was not true. The poor man had no learning. He had never read many books. And yet, the most learned man in the land could not have given the infidel a better answer than this poor man did. Pointing to a Bible that lay on the table before him, he said to the infidel: 'Massa, you say dat Book is not true. Dat Book *is* true. I was once a drunkard, a liar, a blasphemer. I used to steal, and quarrel with everybody. But dat Book made a great change in me. It taught me to be honest, and true, and gentle, and sober. If dat Book was not true, if it was a bad Book, it would never make a bad man good.'

That was an excellent answer. A bad book may make a good man bad, but it will not make a bad man good. The men who read the Bible and obey it, are the best men in the world; but the men who do not read it, or who hate and despise it, are the worst. Wherever this Book goes, and is rightly used, the dew of God's blessing goes with it, and this makes men useful and happy. It promotes the growth of every good thought and feeling in their minds and hearts, just as the dew in the garden causes the flowers to grow. It was the dew of God's blessing on his reading of the Bible which made such a change in the man of whom we have just spoken, and which caused him to grow in the grace, and knowledge, and love of God.

I have only one other illustration of this part of our subject. We may call it—

DO YOUR BEST.

'When I was a little boy,' said a gentleman one day to a friend with whom he was talking, 'I paid a visit to my grandfather. He was an aged man, and wore a black velvet cap, and knee-breeches with large silver buckles at the knees. When I went to say good-bye to him, he took me between his knees, kissed me kindly, and then laying his hand on my head, he said,—

'"My dear boy, I have only one thing to say to you. Will you try and remember it?"

'I looked him in the face, and said, "I will, grandpa."

'"Well," said he, "it is this: whatever you have to do, *always do the best you can.*"

'This, in fact,' said the gentleman, 'was my grandfather's legacy to me. It was worth more than thousands of gold and silver. I never forget his words, and have always tried to act upon them. After reaching home, my father gave my brother Marcus and myself some beds to weed in the garden. It was Saturday afternoon, and we had arranged to go a-fishing. We were greatly disappointed, and not in a very good humour. Marcus fretted and worried, and didn't half do his work. I began in the same way. But presently I remembered grandpa's advice, and resolved to follow it. I went to work and did my best. After awhile, father came out to see how we were getting on. I never shall forget how pleased he looked, when he saw the beds that I had weeded; nor the sixpence that he slipped into my hand, as he said, "Well done, Willie; now you can go and play." Marcus had to drudge over his beds all the afternoon. He got no play, no praise, and no sixpence.

'At fifteen I was sent to the academy. I followed my grandfather's advice there. It soon put me at the head of my class, and kept me there.

'Before my year was out, my mother had three offers of places for me. One of these was from the best merchant in the village. In going into business, I followed grandfather's advice, and always did the best I could. This made me successful. When I joined the church I tried to do the Lord's work as I did my own, and the same rule has made me successful there too.'

This gentleman is one of the best business men in the place where he lives, one of the best citizens, one of the best officers of the church, one of the best friends of the poor, one of the best neighbours, fathers, husbands, friends; he is universally loved and respected. And what was the secret of his success? It was the dew of God's blessing resting on him, as he faithfully followed his grandfather's advice. This led to the growth of his character from the unknown little boy, to the successful man of business—the earnest, happy, useful Christian. Let every boy and girl follow this example, and always resolve to do the best you can. The first blessing which follows from the dew is *life and growth.*

The second blessing which follows from the dew is—BEAUTY.

If we walk through a field in which the grass is withered, or through a garden in which all the flowers are dead, everything will seem dreary and desolate. But if we walk through a field where the grass is growing finely, or through a garden where all the flowers are blooming brightly, how much beauty we shall see, on every hand! And if we see the dewdrops trembling on the leaves of the flowers, and sparkling like rainbows, as the sunbeams shine on them, this will greatly increase the beauty of the scene.

Now the Church is God's garden; and His people are the flowers growing in it. His grace, or blessing, is the dew that rests on these flowers. And the effect of this dew upon them is, not only to promote their life, and growth, as we have seen, but also to increase their beauty. Jesus, our glorious Saviour, is the model of beauty, in the heavenly world, as well as in this. And, as the dew of His blessing rests on His people, it makes them more and more like Himself; and the more they become like Him, the greater their beauty will be. Let us look at some illustrations of the beauty that appears in those on whom the dew of God's blessing is resting, making them more like Jesus.

Our first story may be called—

A BEAUTIFUL TEMPER.

This story is told of a faithful minister of the gospel, who had a large share of the dew of God's blessing resting upon him, and was greatly beloved by all who knew him.

One spring he had been laying out and ornamenting the grounds about his house. He had spared no expense or labour, and they were put in the nicest possible order. But on the very first night after the work was finished, with its grading, and terracing, and sodding, and planting, a herd of wandering swine got into the grounds. They spent the greater part of the night there. Their busy snouts were hard at work rooting up the beds of the garden which had just been nicely dressed, and the new made grass plots were all turned upside down. Everything was wrecked and ruined. When the good old Doctor stepped out on his porch the next morning, to take a little walk before breakfast, he saw at a glance all the mischief which had been done. This would have made many a man very angry; and he would have been tempted to say some sharp things. But it was different with this good minister. Of course he was truly sorry when he saw what had been done. He stood for a moment, and looked calmly at the ruin wrought upon his grounds; and then, without speaking one angry word, as he turned to go into the house again, he quietly said, 'Well, you never can lay dirt so as to suit a hog!'

Certainly it was a beautiful temper which that good old minister had. And here we see the effect which the dew of God's blessing had upon him.

Our next story may be called—

ONE TO BE TRUSTED.

A New York captain, whose ship was fastened to the wharf, had to be absent from the city for several days. His mates were away too, and there was no one he could trust with the charge of the vessel. A man by the name of John, was recommended to him as a fit person. But the captain knew nothing of him, and had no confidence in him. He thought every sailor would steal, when he got a chance. But he could do no better, so he engaged John to keep watch for him, but he locked up everything on board the ship, because he was afraid to trust him.

Early the next morning, before leaving the city, he

thought he would just step on board the ship to see how things looked. So he went on board, and walked quietly to the door of the cabin. There was a pane of glass in that door. He looked through the window, and what should he see, but John on his knees, with an open Bible before him. He had been reading the Bible, and was then engaged in prayer. The captain was delighted. He thought that was one of the pleasantest sights he had ever seen. It relieved him of all fear about the ship. The captain walked about the deck till John came out. Then he went up to him, and handing him all the ship's keys said: 'John, you may open all the drawers and trunks and air the things in them. Keep a sharp look out, John, for the thieves along the wharves. Have everything snug; and I'll be back in two or three days.'

Then he went off, feeling greatly relieved and comforted by what he had seen of John. The dew of God's blessing was resting on that man, and it was this which made him appear in a light that was so pleasant and beautiful to the captain.

Our next story we may call—

A BEAUTIFUL BOY.

Little Mary was prettily dressed, and was standing in front of their house, waiting for her mother to take her out riding.

A nice tidy boy, though dressed in very plain clothes, was passing by, when the little girl said, 'Come here, boy, and s'ake hands wi' me. I dot a boy dus' like you named Joey.'

The boy laughed, shook hands with her, and said, 'I've got a little girl just like you, only she hasn't any little cloak with pussy fur on it.'

Just then a lady came out of the door of the house,

and said, 'Mary, you musn't play with bad boys on the street.' And looking at the boy, she said, 'I hope you haven't stolen anything from her. Go right along, and never stop here again, boy.'

On the evening of that day this lady was called downstairs, to speak to a little boy. He was very neatly dressed, and stood with his cap in his hand. The lady saw, in a moment, that it was the same boy who had been there in the morning, and to whom she had spoken so sharply.

'I came to tell you, ma'am,' said he, 'that I am not a bad boy. I go to Sunday school; and help my mother all I can. I never tell lies, nor quarrel, nor say bad words, and I don't like a lady to call me bad names, and ask me if I have stolen anything from her little girl.'

'I'm very glad you're so good,' said the lady, laughing at the boy's earnestness. 'Here's a shilling for you.'

'Thank you, ma'am, but I don't want that,' said the little fellow, lifting up his head very high. 'My father works in the foundry, and has lots of money. You have a boy bigger than I, haven't you?'

'Yes, but why do you ask that?'

'Does he know the ten commandments?'

'I'm afraid not very well!'

'Can he say the Sermon on the Mount, and the Twenty-third Psalm, and the Golden Rule?'

'I'm very much afraid he can't,' said the lady, smiling at the little boy.

'Doesn't he ride on his pony on Sunday, instead of going to church?'

'I'm afraid he does, but he ought not,' said the lady, blushing a little.

'Mother don't know that I've come here,' said the little fellow, 'but I thought I'd come round and see what kind of folks you are, and—and I guess mother would rather your boy wouldn't come about our door, because she don't like little Susie to talk to bad boys in the street. Good evening, ma'am—' and off the little fellow went.

Now the dew of God's blessing was resting on that boy. It enabled him to teach that lady a beautiful lesson, and set her boy a beautiful example.

I have one other illustration of this part of our subject. We may call it—

WHITER THAN SNOW.

In one of the beautiful palaces of England, there lived a nobleman, who was not a Christian, and never went to church. He had a lovely little girl, about six years old. Her name was—Alberta. She was the delight of her father's heart.

One day she was alone with him in his library, engaged in play. Presently she stopped her play, and looking earnestly into her father's face, she said, 'Papa, do you know anything whiter than snow?'

'No, my darling,' said he, 'there isn't anything whiter than snow.'

'Oh! but there is,' said the child.

'Pray what is it, my child?' he asked.

'Father, the soul washed in the blood of the Lord Jesus is whiter than snow.'

The nobleman was surprised and displeased at this. He had never taught his child anything about religion, and did not want to have any one else teach it to her.

'Who taught you that, my child?' he asked.

'Mary, my nurse,' was her reply.

Her father rang a bell, and presently a servant appeared. 'Tell Mary, the nurse of Alberta, to come here at once.'

The nurse came. She was asked if she had taught Alberta this about the blood of Christ. She admitted that she had. Then the nobleman said, 'I cannot allow you, or any one else, to undertake to teach my child such things as this.' And then taking out his watch he said, 'You can go to the steward, and get the wages due to you, and then leave the castle within an hour.'

Not long after this, a royal prince came to spend a few days with this nobleman. It was the occasion of great rejoicing to all in the castle. One day during this visit, the prince was sitting with the nobleman in his library engaged in conversation. Alberta was there playing with her doll. The Prince called her to him, and taking her on his knee, had a talk with her. Presently she fixed her large eyes on his face, and said, 'Prince, do *you* know anything that is whiter than snow?'

'No, dear,' said he, 'I have never heard of anything whiter than snow; have you?'

'Oh yes, Prince; *the soul washed from its sins in the blood of Jesus Christ is whiter than snow.*' There was silence in that library after this. Neither the Prince nor the nobleman had a word to say. But the repeating of these words by his child had a strange effect on Alberta's father. It led him to think and pray over it. Before long he became a Christian. Alberta's nurse, Mary, was brought back to the castle. She was restored to her old place, and told that she might talk to the dear child about Jesus as much as she pleased.

We think of the snow, in its purity, as one of the most beautiful things in the world. And so it is. But yet, the soul that has been washed in the blood of Jesus is whiter, and more beautiful than snow.

The second blessing that follows from the dew is *beauty*.

The third blessing that follows from the dew is—FRUITFULNESS.

In the garden we find bushes and plants that bear fruits

of various kinds. Strawberries, and raspberries, and currants, and gooseberries, and other kinds of fruit are found there. And these depend largely on the dew that falls on them every night, to enable them to bring forth plenty of fruit. The dewdrops moisten the soil in which those plants are growing, and also the leaves, and buds, and berries, which make up the plants themselves, and so increase very much the amount of fruit which they bear. If there were no dew on those plants, they would wither, and become weak and sickly, and bear little or no fruit. But plenty of dew falling upon them will greatly increase their fruitfulness.

And just so, in the garden of God's Church, the dew of His blessing causes the souls of His people to bring forth plentifully the fruits of good works.

The Apostle Paul was the most fruitful plant ever found in this garden. From the time that he became a Christian, until the day of his death, he was actively engaged in all sorts of good works. He went on one missionary journey after another, going all round the world, and preaching Jesus Christ to souls that were perishing. And it was the dew of God's blessing which made him so fruitful in good works. And what this dew did for St. Paul, when he was on our earth, eighteen hundred years ago, it can do for all God's people now. Let us look at some examples of the fruitfulness caused by this dew.

Our first example may be called—

SOWING AND REAPING.

The Rev. Joseph Entwistle was a very faithful minister of the gospel in England. One day he was walking along one of the principal streets in Liverpool, when a tall, clerical looking gentleman placed his hand upon his shoulder and said, 'Do you remember me, Mr. Entwistle!'

'No, sir,' was his reply. 'I have no recollection of ever having seen you before.'

'Well, sir, don't you remember, many years ago, walking on the terrace of the Kingswood School, and teaching a little boy these lines—

> '"Whate'er thy age would reap, thy youth must sow,
> For the great seedtime of thy life is now."'

'Oh! yes, sir; I remember that, very well.'

'Well, sir, I'm that boy. Those lines were a great blessing to me. They led to my conversion. And now, I am a minister of the gospel.'

What a small seed it was which that good minister was sowing when he taught that boy those two lines! But the dew of God's blessing rested on that seed, and made it very fruitful. All the good that followed from the life and labours of that minister, would be the harvest that grew up from that one little seed.

Our next illustration may be called—

THE FRUIT OF ONE MAN'S LABOURS.

Some years ago a young business man was converted from infidelity, by the efforts of a Christian lady. He made up his mind to study for the ministry. But, while going on with his studies, he resolved to try and make himself useful, by working for Jesus. He gave up his Sundays, and the time not devoted to study, to try and do some good in a poor and neglected neighbourhood. There was no church, and no Sunday school, in that part of the city, and no place in which to hold one. At last he found an unfinished house, and succeeded in renting the third storey of it. He had it plastered, and fitted up for a Sunday school.

Very few persons came at first. But he went on, diligently visiting through the neighbourhood, and earnestly praying for the dew of God's blessing to rest on his labours. The attendance on his school steadily increased, till finally it was crowded.

Then he went to work, to try and build a church in that neighbourhood. By his persevering efforts the money was raised, and a neat substantial stone church was built. Then a parsonage was put up; and now a large congregation of the poor meet regularly there to worship God, and give evidence in their daily lives that they are His true and faithful servants.

And all around that church dark homes have been brightened, and multitudes, once living in sin and misery, are now happy and useful in serving God. And all this good fruit was brought forth by the dew of God's blessing on the labours of that one man.

I have one other illustration of this part of our subject. We may call it—

ONE WOMAN'S WORK.

Some years ago Mrs. Bartlett, an earnest Christian woman, was asked to take temporary charge of a class of three young women in the Sunday school connected with Mr. Spurgeon's Church in London. It was a humble work, but she was afraid to undertake it, and only consented to do so when very much pressed. She was not a woman of much education or talent. But she was a Christian of deep and earnest piety. At the close of the first month, she had been so successful that they urged her to become the permanent teacher of her class. She consented to do so. Her class increased in numbers. Before long it was necessary to get a larger room for her. This room would hold fifty scholars. This was soon filled. Then they got her one that would hold eighty. In a little while this was crowded full. Finally they gave her the use of the lecture-room connected with Mr. Spurgeon's Church. This would hold a thousand people, and there this class increased, till it numbered near seven hundred members. During the time in which Mrs. Bartlett was teaching that class, nearly a thousand of its members joined themselves to different churches in London, and became earnest and devoted servants of Christ. This faithful teacher continued her work till she was sixty-nine years old. Then her labours on earth were ended, and she entered into 'the rest that remaineth for the people of God.' And even during her last sickness, she was thinking all the time about her class. As she remembered, one and another, who had not been converted, she was heard praying for them individually: 'Lord, save her. Save her now.' And then as she thought of the whole class, her prayer would be—'Lord, bless and save them all. Save them all, for Jesus' sake. Amen.'

Who can tell the amount of good that was done by the labours of that one faithful Christian woman? But all this fruitfulness was brought forth by the dew of God's blessing that rested on her work.

We have spoken of three blessings which follow from the natural dew that rests on the plants in our garden; and of the corresponding blessings that follow from the dew of God's grace as it rests upon the souls of His people. The first of these is *life and growth;* the second is *beauty;* and the third is *fruitfulness.* Let our earnest prayer be, for the promised dew of God's blessing to rest upon our souls —and then growth, and beauty, and faithfulness, will mark all that we may be permitted to do for Him.

X.

THE PROMISED GRACE.

'*My grace is sufficient for thee.*'—2 Cor. xii. 9.

VERY few of 'the exceeding great and precious promises' of God's word have been oftener used, or found more profitable than this. Our present course of sermons on 'Bible Promises,' would hardly be complete, if *this* were left out.

If you and I could enter heaven, and talk with the people of God, in the happiness which they are enjoying there; and if we should ask, one after another of them, to tell us about some of the trials they had met with while on earth, and of the comfort they had found from this promise when passing through those trials, what interesting stories they would tell us! It is eighteen hundred years ago since this promise was given to the Apostle Paul. And in all those many years, there has never been a single day in which one or more of God's people have not been helped, and comforted, by this precious promise. And what this promise has done for them, it is able to do for us. If we only remember it, and use it, as God intends that we should do, we shall find it a great help to us.

Our sermon to-day is about—*the promised grace.*

And if we use this promise, in the right way, we shall

find that the grace of which it speaks will be sufficient to do *three* great things for us.

In the first place, it will give us—STRENGTH FOR DUTY.

And this is what we need all the time. Our Saviour said to His disciples—'Without Me ye can do nothing.' This is just as true of each of us, as it was of them. Of ourselves we cannot think a good thought. We cannot put into our hearts one good desire. And if that desire were there, we have no power, of ourselves, to carry it out, or bring it to good effect. When left to ourselves we are not able to speak good words, or to perform good works of any kind. And it is just this fact which makes the promise of our text so precious and valuable to us. When God says, 'My grace is sufficient for thee,' He means that it will supply all our need, and enable us to do our duty, in a way that we never could do without that grace. In the beautiful language of one of the Collects of the Prayer Book, it will—'help us to think those things that are good, and also to perform the same.'

The Apostle Paul said, 'I can do all things through Christ strengthening me.' He meant by this that the grace of God was sufficient to enable him to do his duty, in all things. And the grace that was sufficient for him will be sufficient for you and me. Here are some illustrations of this part of our subject. The first story shows us how—

THE GRACE OF GOD HELPED A BOY TO DO HIS DUTY.

A boy named Charles, on leaving home to go into business, had a companion who slept in the same room with him, and who never said his prayers at night. This boy's name was John.

The first night Charles was there, he did not know what to do about saying his prayers. Satan whispered to him, 'Never mind about kneeling down. You can pray in your heart. God will hear it just as well. Or you can wait till you get into bed and say your prayers. Then no one will see you, and it will be just the same as if you were on your knees.'

But Charles had been taught by a pious mother, now in heaven, always to kneel down by his bedside to say his prayers; and he felt that it was his duty to do so.

He got over the difficulty the first night by waiting till his companion was in bed, and asleep, and then he knelt down and said his prayers as usual. But the next night he got first to his room, and being alone he knelt down to pray. While he was thus engaged he heard the footsteps of his companion coming up the stairs, and hesitated about what he should do. The tempter said to him, 'Get up; he'll see you and laugh at you, and you'll never hear the end of it.' But conscience said to him, 'No; your duty is to stay on your knees and pray on. And the grace of God was sufficient to help him to do his duty. This was a blessing to Charles through all his after-life. He learned to be always decided in doing his duty. And his example that night was a blessing to his companion. It led him also to kneel down and pray to God.

The late excellent Wm. E. Dodge, of New York, tells the next story. It shows us—

HOW THE GRACE OF GOD HELPED AN ENGINEER TO DO HIS DUTY.

'Some years ago,' says Mr. Dodge, 'while I was Superintendent of the Fourteenth Street Church Sunday School, I had a most faithful teacher, who was an engineer on the New Haven Railroad, and who ran the eight o'clock morning express, leaving daily, except Sunday. One winter there had been a heavy snowstorm all Saturday. On Sunday morning the snow was very deep all along the road. About half-past eight o'clock the superintendent of the road sent word to this engineer to come and get out his engine, and help to clear the road. He sent back word that he was just going to Sabbath school and could not come. The messenger was ordered to return and say that he must come at once and get out his engine. The reply he sent back was: "I am only engaged to run the daily express. I am ready at all times to do anything else the Superintendent may require; but now my duty to God calls me to my Sunday-school class, and I dare not run an engine on the Sabbath day."

'When he came to the school that morning I saw he looked anxious,' says Mr. Dodge, 'and as I passed him, he said, "Mr. Dodge, I suppose I have lost my situation on the railroad, because I would not break the Sabbath." Then he told me all about it.

'I said to him, "If you are discharged for such a cause let me know about it, and I will secure you as good a position on the New Jersey Central Railroad. But you go in the morning to the Superintendent, and politely and frankly state your case to him. I know him very well, and I don't think you will have any trouble."

'I did not see this engineer again,' says Mr. Dodge, 'till he came to school the next Sabbath morning. I asked him what was the result; his reply was, "I went, as you suggested, and began to explain, when he stopped me and said, 'I understand and appreciate your conscientious feelings. You shall never again be called upon to run your engine on Sunday.'"

'And that conscientious Sunday-school teacher,' said Mr. Dodge, 'is now receiving higher wages than any other engineer on that road.'

Now it was the grace of God which helped that man

to do his duty. And in doing it he found out how true it is, as David says, that, 'in keeping God's commandments there is great reward.'

Here is one more story to illustrate this part of our subject. It shows us how—

A YOUNG CHRISTIAN GIRL WAS HELPED, BY THE GRACE OF GOD, TO DO HER DUTY.

She had charge of the children in a very wealthy family. One day she called on the minister whose church she attended, and said,—

'I have called to tell you, sir, that I think of leaving my present situation.'

'Why so?' inquired her pastor.

'Why, sir, my mistress pays no attention to the children, but leaves the entire care of them with me, and I feel that it is more than I can stand. Sometimes I never see her for three or four days together. She is what is called a fashionable woman; and is constantly going to balls, and operas, and theatres. She leaves the entire charge of four young children to me, and seldom takes any notice of them.'

After thinking over the matter a little, the minister advised his young friend not to leave her situation. 'True,' said he, 'your duty there is very trying. But I am sure that God will help you to do your duty, and will bless you in doing it.'

The minister's advice was taken, and the young woman remained in her situation.

About a year after this, she called on her minister again. Now she was dressed in black, and in a few words she told how her mother had died, and that her father, a small farmer in the country, needed her help in his home.

'For this reason,' she said, 'I am going to leave my place, sir. I have called to say good-bye, and to thank you for the advice you gave me when I called on you before. I am sure, sir, you will be glad to hear of the change that has taken place in my mistress within the last few months. She has given up going to balls and theatres. She has become a Christian, and joined the church. They now have family worship in their home; and in the care of her children, and her servants, she is entirely different from what she used to be. Before I left my mistress called me aside, and said, "Alice, I am very sorry you have to leave. Of course, under the circumstances, I can say nothing against it. But, before you go, I want to tell you what a blessing your consistent example and Christian life have been to me. It is this which has led to the great change you have seen in my family." I only mention this, sir,' said the young woman very modestly, 'because I think you ought to know what good has followed from the advice you gave me.'

And here we see how sufficient the grace of God was to enable this Christian girl to do her duty. And if we ask God for it, we shall find that it will always give us *strength for duty.*

But the second thing that the grace of God will do for us, is to give us—COMFORT IN TROUBLE.

The Apostle Paul was in trouble when he wrote the words of the text. He tells us that he had 'a thorn in his flesh,' which occasioned him great inconvenience. We can easily understand this. If you, or I, should run a thorn or splinter into our hand or foot, and be unable to get it out, we know very well what the consequence would be. It would swell up, and become inflamed and painful, and would cause us a great deal of trouble. Now St. Paul had an affliction of some kind, which he compares to such a thorn. He does not tell us what it was, and it is impossible for us to decide. Many different opinions have been held about it. Some have supposed it was a trouble about the eyes; or a bodily weakness of some kind, on account of which his enemies ridiculed and made sport of him.

But the apostle also speaks of it as 'a messenger of Satan,' that was allowed, as he says, 'to buffet him.' To buffet means to strike, or to beat. And it would be a very troublesome thing to have some one hitting or beating us all the time. Some have supposed from this that the apostle's 'thorn in the flesh,' was some trouble in the church at Corinth, growing out of the false doctrines that were taught there. But it is impossible to tell exactly what this 'thorn in the flesh' was. We only know that it was something which occasioned St. Paul a great deal of trouble. And he tells us that he prayed to the Lord three times to have it removed. The thorn was not taken away, but the answer to his prayer came in the words of our text,—'My grace is sufficient for thee.' This was just as if God had said to him, 'It will be better for you, Paul, not to have your thorn in the flesh taken away, but I will give you all the help and strength you need to enable you to bear it comfortably.' And this is just the way in which God deals with all His people. When we are in any trouble, if we ask God to help us, He will certainly do it; either by removing the trouble, or else by giving us all the grace we need, to comfort us in bearing it. There are many illustrations of the way in which God does this. Let us look at some of them. Our first story may be called—

THE LORD IN ALL, AND ALL IN THE LORD.

'I had in my parish at one time,' said an aged pastor, 'a very wealthy man, who was an earnest Christian, who gave liberally of his abundance to every good cause, and was very happy in his religion.

'But in the course of time, great troubles came upon him. He failed in business, and lost all his property, and was obliged to engage as book-keeper in the large business house which had once been all his own. Still he was as regular as ever at church on Sundays, and at the week-day meetings; was cheerful and pleasant as ever, and no change was seen in him except that he was not able to give as he had formerly done.

'I spoke to him one day,' said his pastor, 'and asked him how he managed to be so cheerful and happy, under all his troubles. We all expected that you would be sad and sorrowful; but you seem brighter and more sunshiny even than you used to be before these troubles came upon you. How is this?'

'"Let me tell you how it is," he said, in his own cheerful way. "When I was rich and could get everything that I wished for, or that money could buy, I used to enjoy the Lord in all things. But now, since these troubles have come upon me, and my money is all gone, I *enjoy all things in the Lord.* I find His grace sufficient for me. It supplies all my wants, and makes me so happy, that I have to be praising and glorifying His name from day to day."'

Like St. Paul, that good Christian merchant did not find his thorn in the flesh taken away; but, like the great apostle, he found the grace of God sufficient to comfort him in his trouble.

Our next illustration may be called—

THE PASTOR OF KÖNIGSBERG.

During the great fire which nearly destroyed Königsberg in the year 1764, a pastor of that city, ninety years old, lost his church, his house, his valuable library, and all his worldly goods. One of his grandsons ran up-stairs during the fire and carried the old man out on his shoulders.

Once, when asked by a friend to tell him the result of his long and varied experience of life, he said:

'I have been reading and meditating on the ninety-first Psalm. I have found every statement it contains to be true, and every promise in it sure. I have lived in times of pestilence; but during those times I have dwelt in the secret place of the Most High, and have abode under the shadow of the Almighty.

'I have passed through times of war and bloodshed; but His faithfulness has always been my shield and buckler. I was in danger from the fire, but He gave His angels charge over me, and they bore me up in their hands and brought me safely through. In all the many troubles of my long life, His promises have never failed. His grace has always been sufficient for me. There remains but one promise yet to be fulfilled. For this I am now waiting. It is that in which He says, "I will show him My salvation."'

What a beautiful illustration that old pastor's experience affords of the sufficiency of God's grace!

I have one other illustration to give of this part of our subject. We may call it—

THE HAPPY WOODCUTTER.

In these days of missionary labours, we hear incidents from all parts of the world of the power of the gospel to help and comfort those who are in trouble. The story I have now to tell comes from a place called Adana, in the interior of Turkey. There was a great religious interest prevailing in the mission there. The missionary had a visit from a poor native, who had lately joined the Mission Church. After asking him a variety of questions, he made this statement:—

'I am a poor man. I earn four or five piasters a day by my labour.' (A piaster is a piece of money worth about four or five cents; so that twenty or twenty-five cents a day was all that this poor man could earn.) 'I cut up bushes by the roots,' he went on to say, 'and carry them into the town on my back, and sell them for fire-wood. I am ignorant as well as poor. I cannot read. I went out into the fields to-day to bring in bushes; it was raining; the mud was ankle deep; the wind blew cold from the mountains; I was muddy up to the knees; my thin clothes were wet through,—and yet I went along with my heart so full of joy that I had to sing praises to God all the way.'

'And what is it that gives you so much joy?' asked the missionary.

'Oh, sir, it is *the thought that Christ is with me.* He was with me in the rain, and the mud, and the cold wind. He is with me in my labour and my poverty. He is here in my heart. He helps me in my work; He comforts and cheers me. He loves me and I love Him. It was this thought which sent me along the road to-day, singing God's praises as I went. And it is this thought which makes me so anxious that all my countrymen should learn to know and love this precious Saviour, that He may make them as happy as He has made me.'

Here we see how true it is that the grace of God is sufficient to give us comfort in all our troubles.

There is one other thing for which the grace of God is sufficient, and that is to give us—VICTORY OVER OUR ENEMIES.

We can have no better illustration of the precious promise now before us than we find in the Apostle Paul, to whom it was first given. All through his long life of faithful service to his God and Saviour, he found the grace of God sufficient for him. It was sufficient to strengthen him for duty; to comfort him in trouble; and to give him victory over his enemies. And a noble victory it was which it gave him! As he went on with his missionary work, travelling from city to city, he knew very well that 'in every place bonds and afflictions awaited him.' 'But none of these things move me,' said he. 'Neither count I my life dear unto myself; so that I may finish my course with joy, and testify the gospel of the grace of God.' And as he drew near to the close of his ministry, we find the spirit of victory within him expressing itself thus: 'I am now ready to be offered, and the time of my departure is at hand. I have fought a good fight, I have finished my course, I have kept the faith: henceforth there is laid up for me a crown of righteousness' (2 Tim. iv. 6–8). What a glorious victory the great apostle had gained over his enemies when he could thus speak! And the grace which was sufficient to secure such a victory to him, will do the same for you and me, and for all the people of God. This grace, we are told, will make us not only conquerors, 'but more than conquerors through Him who has loved us.' Let us look at some illustrations of the victory which God's grace gives to His people, under all their difficulties. Our first story may be called—

VICTORY OVER BLINDNESS.

One of the most famous sculptors ever known in France was named Vidal. When he was a young man, and getting to be a very skilful artist, he was taken with a very severe spell of sickness, which injured his eyesight, and left him entirely blind. This was a great blow to him, and made him feel very sad. He was very unwilling to think of giving up his great life work as an artist; but what could he expect to do without the use of his eyes? For a while he clung to the idea that he might finally get over this trouble; and, in spite of all that the doctor said to the contrary, he still kept on trying one thing after another, in the hope of regaining the use of his eyes. But at last he became satisfied that it was no use to try for this any longer. Then he gave it up, and sought to be resigned to this great trouble; but it was hard work. One day the doctor said to him:

'My friend, you are blind indeed, but still, I don't want you to give up the idea of being an artist. You will find that though you have lost the use of one sense, viz. your eyesight, yet this very loss will help to sharpen, and quicken your other senses, and make them more useful than they were when you could see. This will especially be the case with the sense of feeling; and if you persist in the effort to cultivate this sense, with half the courage and perseverance with which you have tried to recover your eyesight, you may become as good a sculptor, without the use of your eyes, as ever you could have been with them.'

This comforted and encouraged the poor artist very much. He resolved to see what he could do, and asked God's blessing on his efforts. He went on patiently and perseveringly, trying to cultivate the sense of feeling, or touch. After considerable practice, when he found that he could, as he said, 'see a little with his fingers,' his joy was very great. 'Perhaps,' said he, 'the good Lord will give me ten eyes instead of two'—referring to the use of his fingers—'and then, how thankful I shall be!'

And it turned out just so. God's blessing, on his patient industry, was sufficient to give him the victory over the loss of his eyesight. He could go to work on a block of marble, with his mallet and his chisel; and instead of looking at it with his eyes, he could feel it with his fingers, and tell exactly by his touch, what was needed to be done. He became one of the most skilful and famous artists in France. And by the use of his fingers he could make a better statue than any other sculptor could make by the use of his eyes. Certainly the grace of God was sufficient to give him the victory over the loss of his eyesight.

Our next story illustrates the sufficiency of God's grace to give—

VICTORY OVER THE USE OF TOBACCO.

In a large manufacturing town in Connecticut, there lived a blacksmith, whose name was Johnson. He had for years been a rough wicked man, and a hard drinker; but finally he became a Christian, and joined the church.

At first he seemed to grow in grace, and to be a bright, happy Christian. But after awhile he did not appear to be doing so well. It was evident that there was something wrong about him. The pastor of the church tried in vain to find out what was the matter with him.

One day, in passing down the street, he saw Johnson coming out of a cigar store, with a great lump of chewing tobacco in his hand, of which he was taking a large bite. The minister was sorry to see it, and felt sure that this was the difficulty in Johnson's way.

In the church to which he belonged, they were in the habit of holding a weekly meeting for prayer. In those meetings the members of the church were accustomed to make short addresses. During one of the meetings the blacksmith rose to say a few words. He told how much the Lord had done for him, and what he was trying to do for the Lord: 'My houses and lands,' said he, 'I've laid on the altar; my wife and children I've laid on the altar; my—'

'Brother Johnson,' asked an old deacon, 'have you laid your tobacco on the altar?'

The blacksmith took his seat. He was not prepared to answer that question, and had nothing more to say.

For several weeks after this, the blacksmith was not present at that meeting. After awhile, however, he went again. In the course of the meeting he rose up to speak. He was repeating what he had said at the previous meeting: 'I've laid my houses and lands on the altar; I've laid my wife and children on the altar; I've—'

'Have you laid your tobacco on the altar?' asked the old deacon again.

The blacksmith turned, and there was a new light in his eyes, as he answered:

'Yes, brother, thank God, I *have* laid my tobacco on the altar. And now I feel that I can praise God with my whole heart. It was very hard to give it up. I made all sorts of excuses. I found I could not do it myself; so I asked the Lord to help me. I had prayed before for a clean heart, and now I prayed for a clean mouth. The Lord has heard my prayer. His grace was sufficient for me. It has given me the victory over the habit of using tobacco.'

I have only one other story in connection with this part of our subject. It shows us how the grace of God gave to an engineer—

VICTORY OVER THE LOVE OF DRINK.

The owner of a cotton mill in England, had a large stationary engine for running his mill. The engineer, who had been in his employ for a long time, was taken suddenly ill. A man, who had been employed on a neighbouring railway, was highly recommended to him as a skilful engineer. 'His services to us have been invaluable,' said the Superintendent of the road, to the owner of the mill. 'He is the best engineer we ever had, and has saved many lives by his quickness and bravery. He has but one fault, and that is the love of strong drink. He will not let liquor alone, and so we have discharged him. You cannot depend on him for more than five days at a time. On Saturday he always goes off on a spree.'

But the owner of the mill could not afford to let his work stand still. 'And so,' as he said to a friend, 'in spite of this discouraging report, I hired the man. I thought I would watch him carefully, and hoped he might do better. During the first few days that he was working for me, I often passed through the engine-room to see how things were going. But everything was in the nicest possible order, and the engine was working away as smoothly as clock-work. I was delighted, and only hoped it would continue. When Saturday came I trembled. But it passed quietly by, and on Monday morning he was in his place, perfectly sober. Week after week went on in this way. I asked myself in surprise, over and over again, what was the meaning of that report about his working five days and being drunk two! The answer to my question came out in this way :—

'One day as I was passing through the engine-room he said, "May I speak with you a moment, sir?"

'"Certainly," I said. "But what is the matter, John? Are you out of oil?"

'"No, sir," he replied, "it's about myself I wish to speak."

'"Very well, go on; I shall be glad to hear what you have to say." Then he said :

'"Thirty-two years ago I drank my first glass of liquor;

and for the past ten years, until the last month, no single week has passed by without my being drunk on Saturday night. At times my struggles against the longing for drink have been very earnest. My employers once offered me two hundred pounds, if I would not touch liquor for three months, but I lost it. I tried all sorts of remedies, but in vain. My wife died praying that I might be kept from a drunkard's grave; yet my promises to her were broken within two days of her death. I signed pledges, and joined societies, but it did no good. My employers reasoned with me, and then discharged me, but without effect. *I could not stop*, and I knew it. When I came to work for you, I did not expect to stay more than a week; but now!"—and here the old man's face lighted up with a peculiar smile of joy, as he continued—"now, in this extremity, when I was willing to sell my soul for a glass of rum, I have found a sure remedy! I have gotten the victory over my love of drink!"'

'And pray, John,' said his employer, 'tell me what has given you this victory?'

The engineer picked up a Bible, that lay on the window sill, and turning to the ninth verse of the twelfth chapter of 2nd Corinthians read out the words of our text: '"My grace is sufficient for thee." I asked God to help me, sir, and His grace has given me the victory over my enemy.'

Let us all seek the grace here promised, and we shall find in it the greatest blessing we can have. It will give us *strength for duty; comfort in trouble; and victory over our enemies.* And that which will do all this for us, is a blessing indeed!

XI.

THE PROMISE TO THE RIGHTEOUS.

'*Say ye to the righteous that it shall be well with him.*'—ISA. iii. 10.

OUR sermon to-day will finish the course, which has occupied us for the past winter, on 'Bible Promises.'

The promise which our text brings before us is a very beautiful one, and a very proper one with which to end this course.

'Say ye to the righteous it shall be well with him.' 'The righteous!' This is one of the many names, or titles, applied to God's people in the Bible. It does not mean that they were born righteous; or that they made themselves righteous. We are all born into this world as sinners. But when we repent and turn to Jesus, He pardons our sins, and changes our hearts, and makes us good, or righteous. So this term—righteous, is a proper one for all who are the servants of Jesus.

'Say ye to the righteous—*it*—shall be well with him.' 'It' is a little word of only two letters. What does it mean? We call this little word a pronoun. And generally it is used to represent something that has been spoken of before. For example, suppose I should ask one of you to go into the vestry-room, and get a Bible off the table, and bring '*it*' to me. Then that little 'it' would stand for the Bible you were to bring to me. But nothing has been spoken of, in connection with our text, which can be represented by this little word—'it.' The meaning is different here. And then the question comes up, what is its meaning? The best way I can think of, for answering this question, is by the help of another text of Scripture. In Romans viii. 28, the Apostle Paul tells us that—'All things work together for good to them that love God.' And in the passage of Scripture we have for our present text, the little word—'it'—has the same meaning as the 'all things,' of which the apostle is speaking in the other passage. These two verses, one in the Old Testament, and the other in the New Testament, both teach us the same lesson. When the prophet Isaiah gave the Jews this precious promise—'Say ye to the righteous, *it* shall be well with him;' he was teaching them precisely the same truth which the Apostle Paul was teaching the Christians at Rome, when he said, 'We know that all things work together for good to them that love God.' The 'it' in the one passage, and the 'all things' in the other, have both the same meaning. Let us just make this change in our text, and see how it will read: 'Say ye to the righteous—all things—shall be well with him.'

If you and I are loving and serving Jesus, we are among 'the righteous,' spoken of in our text, and we may regard God as telling us, when we read the words of the text, that the sun which shines on us by day, and the moon and the stars by night; that the seasons as they come and go; and the winds that blow about us; and the rains that descend upon us; that the loss of health, or friends; and every trial or trouble that may come upon us, are only helping to make up this little word—'*it*'—in our text, which God promises 'shall be well with us.' Everything that happens to us is intended by God to help us in serving Him, and in making us more fit for that heavenly home, which He is preparing for us.

Our sermon to-day is about—*the promise to the righteous.* 'Say ye to the righteous it shall be well with him.' And there are *three times* when God will fulfil this promise, and make it well with us.

In the first place, God will make 'it' well with us—IN LIFE.

Every day that we live we may regard God as saying to us—'it shall be well with you.' This does not mean that we shall never have any trials, or troubles; but it means that when trials come, God will turn them into blessings, and make them work together for our good. We may not be able to understand *how* God will bring this all about; but we may feel *perfectly sure* that it will be so. We have God's word of promise for it, and His promise, we know, can never be broken.

Let us look at some illustrations of the way in which this is done. Our first story may be called—

IT'S ALL FOR THE BEST.

When Mary, the daughter of Henry VIII., was Queen of England, a great many good Protestant ministers, and people too, were persecuted, because they would not give up their religion and join the Church of Rome. Some were put in prison, and others were chained to the stake and burned to death. There was then a faithful minister whose name was Bernard Gilpin. He was so fully convinced of the truth which the Bible teaches, both in our text, and in other places, that he was in the habit of saying of everything that happened to him—'It's all for the best.' Well, one time during Queen Mary's bloody reign, he received a summons to go up to London and be tried for his life, by those who were putting the

Protestants to death. When he left home his friends never expected to see him again in this world. But while on his way to London he fell and broke his leg.

Somebody said to him, 'Do you think *this* is all for the best?'

'I've no doubt of it,' said he.

Of course he could not travel with a broken leg. He had to be taken care of, on the road, till his leg got well. This detained him there several months. And while he was waiting thus, Queen Mary died. Her sister Elizabeth became Queen of England. She was a Protestant, and the persecution which had been carried on during the reign of her sister was stopped at once. Mr. Gilpin returned home, as soon as he got well, instead of going to London to be put to death. The breaking of his leg was the means of saving his life. This is a good illustration of our text. It was well for that good minister that his leg was broken.

Our next story may be called—

THE TWO CLERKS.

Two young men went to Boston, and got situations there, in a large wholesale business house. They had both been religiously brought up, and the head of the firm in which they were employed was a Christian. One of these young men was named George Brobson, and the name of the other was James Johnson. They were both professors of religion; but when they entered into business they pursued very different courses, and we shall see that while it was not 'well' with one of them, it was 'well' with the other.

They had not been in Boston long, before they became acquainted with a number of young men, most of whom were not Christians. George and James were boarding at the same house, and sharing the same room. Some of their young friends, whose acquaintance they had formed, got into the habit of calling on them on Sunday mornings. By and by, as they were talking together, the church bells would be heard ringing. And just here, the difference between these two young men first began to show itself. George Brobson had made up his mind always to carry his religion with him, wherever he went, and to be faithful to his duty to God, as well as to men. James Johnson had not made any such resolution. Like many other persons, he was ready to do exactly what those about him did, without stopping to think whether it was right or wrong. On these occasions, as soon as the church bell was heard ringing, George would rise, and excuse himself to his friends, and get ready for church. No matter what they said to him, or how much they laughed at him, he paid no attention to it, but went regularly to church. But it was different with his companion James. He listened to the entreaties of his young friends, and gave up going to church.

He got into the habit of spending his Sundays, with those gay young men, in taking pleasure excursions. And then, on the week-day evenings, they took him to the theatre, and to the drinking saloons. In this way he learned to drink. He became intemperate. Then he lost his situation and had to struggle hard to get a living. He gradually became worse and worse; and at last, when he was out sailing with his companions, one Sunday afternoon, suddenly a storm arose. The boat in which they were sailing was upset. Several of the young men were drowned, and James was one of them. This was his sad end. He was not 'righteous'—and certainly it was not 'well' with him.

But how different it was with his friend George! He was an earnest, faithful Christian. In all his business concerns he was diligent and persevering, and had the entire confidence of the gentlemen who employed him. He rose gradually from one position to another, till he became the head clerk in the establishment.

After serving there for some years, he went into business for himself. He was eminently successful in this, and became one of the richest men in Boston. He was an earnest member of the church to which he belonged, and the superintendent of the Sunday school. He was actively engaged in all sorts of good works; and was greatly loved and honoured by all who knew him. He was indeed a righteous man, and we see how surely the promise of the text was fulfilled in his case; for, in very deed and truth—'*it* was well with him.'

In the first place, God will fulfil this promise, and make it well with us *in life.*

In the second place, God will fulfil this promise, and make 'it' well with us—IN DEATH.

Death is something which must come to all of us, sooner or later. And death is a very solemn thing. It will remove us from all our relatives and friends in this world, and take us into the immediate presence of God. And we know from the Bible, that God feels the greatest interest in the death of His people. David tells us that their death 'is precious in His sight' (Ps. cxvi. 15).

God knows how natural it is for His people to be afraid of death, and therefore He has given us precious promises in His word to take away this fear. One of these was the sweet promise He gave to the patriarch Jacob, when he had that wonderful vision, in which he saw the ladder set up from earth to heaven, with the angels of God, going up and down upon it. We read about this vision in the twenty-eighth chapter of Genesis. Jacob was then starting on a long journey, to make a visit to his uncle Laban. God appeared to him above that ladder, which he saw in his vision; and He promised—'to be with him, and keep him in all places whither he went, and never to leave him till He had done all that He spoken to him of.' This promise had a particular had reference to the journey on which Jacob was then starting. But it was not given to Jacob alone; nor only for that journey which he was then taking. No; but it is a promise for you, and for me, and for all the people of God; and it is intended to apply to the whole journey of life. It is a promise that takes in both our life, and our death. That promise, given to Jacob, shows us that the promise in our present text is intended to follow us in blessing, till we get safe home to heaven. It makes us feel sure that through our whole life 'it shall be well with us;' and then it makes us feel equally sure that 'it will be well with us' in death.

I think it very likely that it was the knowledge which David had, of this promise given to Jacob, that made him feel so comfortable when he thought of dying. See how cheerfully he speaks about it, in the twenty-third Psalm, where he uses this language—'Yea, though I walk through the valley of the shadow of death, I will fear no evil; for Thou art with me; Thy rod and Thy staff, they comfort me.' If we only have God, and His blessed word, to lean upon, as our rod and staff, then indeed, 'it will be well with us' in death, and we need fear no evil, when we think of walking through that dark valley. Now let us look at some examples of the way in which God's people have found it well with them in death. We may begin with one example from the Bible. It is the case of good old Simeon. God had told him that he should not die till he had seen the promised Saviour of the world. And when the parents of the infant Jesus brought Him into the temple, to offer for Him the sacrifice required by the Jewish law, Simeon came in at the same time. God told Him who this infant was. Then he took Him up in his arms, and blessed God, and said, 'Lord, now lettest Thou Thy servant depart in peace, according to Thy word; for mine eyes have seen Thy salvation.' The Saviour of the world had come. Simeon had seen, and embraced Him,—and now, he felt that 'it was well with him' in death. The sight of that gracious Saviour had taken away from him all fear of death. He felt that *now*, he could depart in peace.

And here are some other illustrations of this part of our subject. Our first illustration may be called—

PREPARATION FOR DEATH.

If we wish to have 'it well with us' in death, we must be careful to do our duty faithfully in life.

A lady once asked Mr. Wesley, the celebrated Methodist minister, this question:

'If you knew that you must die at twelve o'clock to-morrow night, Mr. Wesley, how would you spend the time between now and then?'

'Why, just as I intend to spend it now. I should preach this evening at Gloucester, as I have appointed; and then again at eight o'clock to-morrow morning. After that I would ride to Tewkesbury, and preach there in the afternoon, and then go to meet the societies in the evening; and then I would go to the house of the friend with whom I am to stay; I would converse and pray with the family as usual; then I would retire to my room at ten o'clock, and commending myself to my Heavenly Father, lie quietly down to rest and sleep, and —*at twelve o'clock wake up in heaven!*'

That good man certainly felt sure that 'it would be well with him' in death.

Our next illustration may be called—

HAPPY IN DEATH.

A faithful minister of the gospel, who laboured among the poor in London, tells this story :—

'Some time ago I stood by the bedside of a poor young woman. She was suffering from a very painful disease, which was dragging her down to the grave. A little garret room was her only home. And yet, in spite of her deep poverty, and her very great suffering, she was always so peaceful and happy, that her plain room used to make me think of heaven.

'I went in to see her one day, and found her very low. The doctor had been to see her a short time before, and said she could not live through that day.

'"Well, Mary," I said to her, "how are you feeling now?"

'"I am near the end of my journey," was her answer; "and I am finishing my Christian course, just as I began it, years ago, at the feet of Jesus!" And then with a feeble voice, she repeated this verse of one of her favourite hymns—

'"A guilty, weak, and helpless worm,
On Thy kind arms I fall;
Be Thou my strength and righteousness,
My Jesus, and my all."

'Then she closed her eyes, and her happy spirit entered into the presence of that Saviour, "whom having not seen she loved."'

Surely 'it was well with her' in death! And when we think of the comfort she found in Jesus, we may take up the sweet lines which some one has written, and say—

'Oh, trust thyself to Jesus
As thy spirit takes its flight,
From every earthly shadow,
To the land of perfect light.

'That is the hour for feeling
"Christ hath done all for me;"
That is the time for singing,
"He gives the victory."'

A faithful minister of Christ was lying on his death-bed. A brother minister was sitting by his bed-side He saw the dying man's face lighted up with an expression of great joy. 'My brother,' he asked, 'do you already see the golden streets and pearly gates of the New Jerusalem?'

'I do,' was his reply.

'Shall we not engage in prayer?' asked his friend.

'I would rather engage in praise,' was the answer of the dying man.

The closing moments of his passing life were spent in praise. The last words he was heard to utter were: 'Glory, glory! Come, Lord Jesus!' It was well with him in death.

These were the last words of another faithful minister, as he lay upon his death-bed: 'I am happy, I am happy! For the last four days my soul has constantly been in a state of "joy unspeakable, and full of glory." I have done with prayer now; I can love, I can praise, but I cannot pray. "Now Lord, lettest Thou Thy servant depart in peace, according to Thy word; for mine eyes have seen Thy salvation."' It was well with that man in death!

Here is another minister on his death-bed. Listen to his last words:

'I know I am dying; but my death-bed is a bed of roses. I have no thorns planted on my dying pillow.

Heaven is already begun. I die a safe, happy death. Thou, my God, art present; I know, I feel that Thou art here. Precious Jesus! Glory, glory be to God!' It was well with him in death!

'The celestial city is full in my view,' said Dr. Payson on his death-bed.

'This is heaven begun,' were the last words of one dying minister.

'I see the New Jerusalem,' were the last words of another. 'Let me go! Let me go!' And so his ransomed soul entered into the presence of Jesus, and the happy multitudes with Him in heaven.

How truly it may be said of such that it is well with them in death!

In the second place, God fulfils the promise of our text, and makes 'it well with the righteous' *in death.*

In the third place, God will fulfil this promise, and make 'it well with the righteous'—AFTER DEATH.

Death is the end of our present life, but it is only the beginning of the life which is to come. That life will have no end; but will go on for ever and ever. And as we begin that life, when our bodies die, so we must go on, and continue it for all eternity. If 'it is well with us' when we begin that life, then it will be well with us for ever. If it is not well with us when we begin that life, then it never, never can be well with us. But if we only love and serve Jesus, and so are found among 'the righteous,' spoken of in our text, then it will be well with us.' *In life* it will be well with us; *in death* it will be well with us; and it will be well with us *after death.* Then our fortune will be made for this world, and for the world to come. We know nothing about what our state will be after death, except what God has told us in the Bible. As David was thinking of this heavenly state, he said, 'When I awake in Thy likeness I shall be satisfied with it. In Thy presence is fulness of joy, and at Thy right hand there are pleasures for evermore.'

When the Apostle Paul was speaking of this state after death, he said, 'I have fought a good fight; I have finished my course; I have kept the faith: henceforth there is laid up for me a crown of righteousness, which the Lord, the righteous Judge, will give me at that day' (2 Tim. iv. 7).

But the best and fullest description of what the state of the righteous will be, after death, is given us in the last two chapters of the New Testament. There we are told more, about this state, than can be found in all the rest of the Bible put together. There the home, in which the souls of the righteous will live after death, is spoken of as—'a holy city,' which the Apostle John saw 'coming down from God, out of heaven.' Its gates are made of pearl; its walls, and its foundations, are of precious stones; and its streets are of gold, as clear as crystal. And there will be no night there; and no sorrow, nor crying, nor pain, and no more death. And God will wipe away all tears from the eyes of those that dwell there. They will see the face of Jesus, and will walk with Him in white. 'And the Lamb that is in the midst of the throne will feed them, and lead them to the fountains of living waters.' The angels will be our companions there; and we shall all be kings and priests unto God for ever. What a state of happiness that will be! Well might the Apostle Paul speak of it as 'a weight of glory;' 'an eternal weight of glory,' 'far exceeding,' and more than exceeding, all that we can now think of! How much there must be, in the hope of this glorious heaven, awaiting us after death, to give us help and comfort in meeting the duties and bearing the burdens of the present life! The Apostle Paul compares this hope of heaven to an anchor; because, just as the sailor lets go his anchor, when the storm bursts upon him, and this enables his vessel to ride through the storm in safety; so this hope of heaven is like an anchor to the soul of the Christian, keeping it steady, and calm, and happy, while the storms of life are beating around it.

Let us look at some illustrations of the way in which this is done. Our first may be called—

THE CHRISTIAN'S HOPE.

One afternoon a pious lady teacher was returning home from school. Her work that day had been very trying, and discouraging; and as she went slowly on her way, she was feeling very sad and uncomfortable. Just then she passed a little shop, kept by an old negro woman. She was a bright, happy Christian. The hope of heaven was not only like an anchor to her soul, but also like a fountain of blessedness, that was always sending forth its streams to make her cheerful and glad. As that sorrowful teacher went by her shop, the old woman was standing on the pavement, arranging some of her goods; at the same time, in the free and easy way belonging to her, she was carrying on a religious conversation with some one inside of her shop. This person was in trouble, and the old woman was trying to comfort her; and just as the weary feet of that discouraged teacher carried her past the store, she heard these words, which the old darkey was speaking to her friend inside: 'De Massa mighty good to His suff'rin' people. Neber min', honey, He'll gib you Heben bymeby, and dat'll make all straight.'

The troubled teacher heard those words, and they were a great comfort to her. If an angel from heaven had spoken to her, he could not have said anything that would have done her more good. The burden was lifted from her heart, and she went on her way rejoicing.

Our next story may be called—

THE HINDOO CHILD'S HOPE OF HEAVEN.

This story has been put into very simple verse, and I give it you in this form.

'A little heathen child there was
On India's sultry plains,
Where idol temples thickly stand,
And pagan darkness reigns:

'She long was taught to put her trust
In blocks of wood and stone;
To sing their praises, worship them,
And pray to them alone.

'A missionary came at last
To tell of better things;
To tell them of our God of love,
Our own great "King of kings."

'A school was pened, and she went
To learn the way to heaven;
She heard of Jesus, by whose blood
Her sins might be forgiven.

'His Spirit changed her youthful heart,
And filled it with His love:
She longed to see Him, and to dwell
With Him in heaven above.

'One day a grievous sickness came,
And laid this dear child low;
She could not leave her little mat;
To school no more could go.

'The missionary kindly went
To see this little child;
Her sufferings made him very sad;
Yet midst them all, she smiled.

'O listen to her feeble voice,
Now she is called to die,
While pain convulsed her frame, and forced
The tear-drop from her eye.

'Yet not one murmuring word arose
From that once heathen child;
For thoughts of Jesus filled her soul,
So that she sweetly smiled.

'Yes, smiled midst agonizing pain,
And smiled with death in view;
For—"After this is heaven," she said;
And soon she proved it true.'

She felt sure that 'it would be well with her' after death, and this thought cheered, and comforted her amidst all her sufferings.

Our last story may be called—

HEAVEN ON EARTH.

A faithful minister of the gospel gives the following account of a humble Christian woman, who was a member of his church. 'She was,' he said, 'one of the happiest Christians I ever knew. She was very poor, and had nothing to live on but what was given her by the church. She lived in a small room, with very little furniture in it; and yet, when I went to visit her, it always seemed like the gate of heaven to me, because she was so happy and joyful. One day she sent word that she was in trouble, and wished to see me.

'Wondering what could possibly bring any trouble to her, I said, as I entered her humble home, "Well, my good friend, do tell me what is your trouble?" "It is just this," she said, "that I cannot pray any more. I did so want to spend the few days left to me on earth, in praying for my friends. But now, whenever I begin to speak to God, I can do nothing but praise Him; and glory!—glory!—glory!—is all that I can say."'

Truly the hope of heaven was more than an anchor to her soul! How sure she was that 'it would be well with her' after death!

We have spoken of three times when God will fulfil this promise to the righteous; these are—*in life—in death*—and *after death.* Oh, let us be sure that we really love and serve Jesus! Then He will count us among the number of His people, and this precious promise will belong to each of us—'Say ye to the righteous that it shall be well with him.'

SGCB Titles for the Young

Solid Ground Christian Books is honored to be able to offer over a dozen uncovered treasure for children and young people.

Bible Warnings: *Sermons to Children on Dangers that lie along their Path and How to Avoid Them* by Richard Newton is the sequel to *Bible Promises* that you hold in your hand. Fifteen brilliant chapters. Newton at his very best!

The Safe Compass and How it Points: *The Bible the Only Sure Guide to Heaven* by Richard Newton directs children to heaven by the Bible, the only safe guide.

Heroes of the Reformation by Richard Newton is a unique volume that introduces children and young people to the leading figures and incidents of the Reformation. Spurgeon called him, *"The Prince of preachers to the young."*

Heroes of the Early Church by Richard Newton is the sequel to the above-named volume. The very last book Newton wrote introduces all the leading figures of the early church with lessons to be learned from each figure.

The King's Highway: *Ten Commandments to the Young* by Richard Newton is a volume of Newton's sermons to children. Highly recommended!

The Life of Jesus Christ for the Young by Richard Newton is a double volume set that traces the Gospel from Genesis 3:15 to the Ascension of our Lord and the outpouring of His Spirit on the Day of Pentecost. Excellent!

The Child's Book on the Fall by Thomas H. Gallaudet is a simple and practical exposition of the Fall of man into sin, and his only hope of salvation.

The Child's Book on Repentance by Thomas H. Gallaudet is a simple and practical exposition of the Fall of man into sin, and his only hope of salvation.

The Child's Book on the Soul by Thomas H. Gallaudet is a simple and practical exposition of the Fall of man into sin, and his only hope of salvation.

The Child at Home by John S.C. Abbott is the sequel to his popular book *The Mother at Home*. A must read for children and their parents.

My Brother's Keeper: *Letters to a Younger Brother* by J.W. Alexander contains the actual letters Alexander sent to his ten year old brother.

The Scripture Guide by J.W. Alexander is filled with page after page of information on getting the most from our Bibles. Invaluable!

Feed My Lambs: *Lectures to Children* by John Todd is drawn from actual sermons preached in Philadelphia, PA and Pittsfield, MA to the children of the church, one Sunday each month. A pure gold-mine of instruction.

Truth Made Simple: *The Attributes of God for Children* by John Todd was intended to be a miniature Systematic Theology for children. Richard Newton said that Dr. Todd taught him how to teach children. Practical and crystal clear!

The Young Lady's Guide by Harvey Newcomb will speak directly to the heart of the young women who desire to serve Christ with all their being.

The Chief End of Man by John Hall is an exposition and application of the first question of the Westminster Shorter Catechism. Full of rich illustrations.

www.ingramcontent.com/pod-product-compliance
Lightning Source LLC
Chambersburg PA
CBHW022130080426
42734CB00006B/292

* 9 7 8 1 5 9 9 2 5 0 5 7 1 *